# Coaching the 4-4-2

## Zone Play
## The Flat Back Four Defense
## Attacking Schemes

### by Floriano Marziali and Vincenzo Mora

*Published by*
**REEDSWAIN, INC.**

# Library of Congress Cataloging - in - Publication Data

Marziali, Floriano and Mora, Vincenzo
  Coaching the 4-4-2/Floriano Marziali and Vincenzo Mora

ISBN No. 0-9651020-8-4
Library of Congress Catalog Card Number is 97-067975
Copyright © 1997

This book was originally published in Italy by Edizioni Nuova Prhomos.

Reedswain books are available at special discounts for bulk purchase. For details, contact the Special Sales Manager at Reedswain at 1-800-331-5191.

Printed in the United States of America.

REEDSWAIN, INC.
612 Pughtown Road • Spring City PA 19475
1-800-331-5191
Web Site: www.reedswain.com

*Special thanks to all those who have
contributed to this book, in particular:*

Clelio Pagnanelli
Sergio Bugiardini
Gaetano Marini
Luciano Corradini

Fermo, 28th July 1995
Floriano Marziali
Vincenzo Mora

# Table of Contents

# Introduction

**M**any experts have developed in depth the playing formations and the related evolution of the roles of the players. Although the theoretical aspects of zone play are continuously being discussed and investigated, the teaching methods have not yet been addressed as thoroughly. This is the reason why this book has been conceived, its aim is specifically practical, so a "graphic exposition" has been preferred to a theoretical one.

The notions, the principles and the basic and necessary concepts to deal with the "zone" subject have been covered in a simple way, yet enough to frame its main features.

As zone play is basically a defensive strategy, dealing with it inevitably means dealing with aspects related to the opponents' possession of the ball as well. Therefore this book gives primary importance to the treatment of the aspects related to the defensive phase, while also taking into account those related to the possession of the ball for which you will find organized and logical attacks, with examples through easy to follow diagrams.

The following pages intend to be both a useful instrument for those who are about to train a team in the zone play for the first time, and a valid help for those who, experienced in zone play, wish to compare their ideas with ours.

The ideas dealt with in the text are the product of the authors' experimentation and personal interpretation (resulting from the comparison of each other's experiences and knowledge), they are not intended to be the final words and hopefully will provoke more thought.

Finally, we maintain that this work, thanks to its particular plan, can be useful to a vast number of people: coaches of young players and professional coaches, players young and old, and, as a whole, to all those who wish to enter the marvelous world of the zone play.

*The authors*

# Symbols

| | |
|---|---|
| **C** | Coach |
| ● | Ball |
| ●———→● | Passing of the ball |
| ⑥ | Player/s to train |
| **D** | Opponent/s |
| ⑧● | Player with the ball to train |
| **D**● | Opposing player with the ball |
| **b.f.** | Player with the ball |
| ⑨●〰→ | |
| ⑨●〰→⑨¹● | Ball guidance |
| ②--→ | |
| --→② | Movement without the ball |
| ②--→②¹ | |
| ⑪ | Temporary position |

# 1

# Specific Features of the Zone Play

## Arranging the Players According to a 4-4-2 Pattern

In diagram 1 you can find the arrangement of the players on the field according to the zone 4-4-2 pattern, which we would like to examine closely.

| Abbreviations of the Players Positions | | |
|---|---|---|
| 1 = P | Goalkeeper |
| 2 = R.S.B. | Right side back |
| 3 = L.S.B. | Left side back |
| 4 = R.C.M. | Right central midfielder |
| 5 = L.C.B. | Left central back |
| 6 = R.C.B. | Right central back |
| 7 = R.S.M. | Right side midfielder |
| 8 = L.C.M. | Left central midfielder |
| 9 = F | Forward |
| 10 = L.S.M. | Left side midfielder |
| 11 = F | Forward |

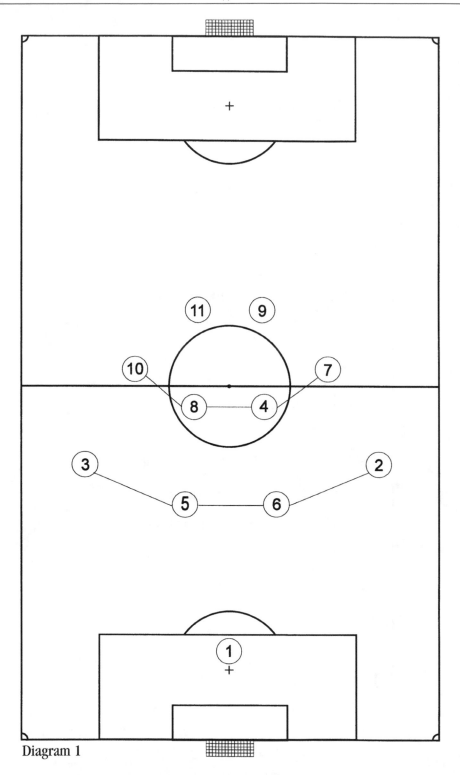

Diagram 1

# The 4-4-2 Pattern Zone Play

Zone play can be defined as mainly defensive tactics aiming at regaining possession of the ball; in this context the opposing player with the ball MUST HAVE THE IMPRESSION THAT HE IS PLAYING AGAINST 11 PLAYERS. As a consequence, in relation to the position of the player with the ball and of the ball itself, each single player must cover a certain space (zone) through zone-marking (a kind of man-marking, but not systematically performed on the same player) also referred to as marking in advance.

In diagram 2 the field has been divided into four zones, called A, B, C, and D; zones B and C are narrower than A and D because, as they are in the middle, they are a major source of danger. This division is necessary from a teaching point of view and has been made to show in which zones the four backs and the four midfielders can move. There are no fixed rules for the forwards; neverthe-less they have zones of responsibility when defending, according to the same principle used for the backs and the midfielders.

To zone-cover, each player must cover his space (his zone) and, if needed, one of the adjoining zones. So, the Left Side Back and the Left Side Midfielder must cover zone "A" and, if needed, zone "B". The Right Side Back and the Right Side Midfielder must take care of zone "D" and, in case of necessity, of zone "C", while the Left Central Back and the Left Central Midfielder must take care of zone "B" and, if needed, of zones "C" and "A". Finally, the Right Central Back and the Right Central Midfielder must cover zone "C" and, in case of necessity, zones "B" and "D". The two forwards, number 11 and 9, could cover the central zones, that is zone "B" and zone "C", so as to "push" the opponents to start the action on the sides, where it is less difficult to press and double-mark.

Forward number 11 should cover zones "B", "C" and "A", while number 9 should cover zones "C", "B" and "D". The coach will decide the covering move-ments of the forwards according to their characteristics, the tactics to use to regain possession of the ball and the skill of the opponents.

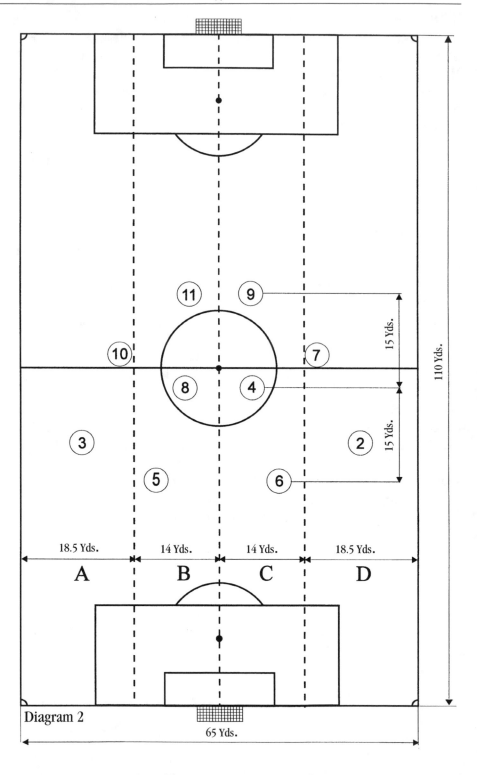

Diagram 2

# Positioning

**In the zone play the back must cover a determined space, he must be POSITIONED so that he can see the BALL and HIS GOAL and must BE PLACED, OR IN A POSITION TO GET HIMSELF PLACED, in between the opponent and HIS OWN GOAL.**

*In this context, the back must be able to man-mark or to mark in advance the opponent playing in his zone of responsibility; the longer the distance between the player with the ball and the marked opponent, the sharper the advance.* To mark in advance means that the back must be in a position to either intercept the ball or place himself between the opponent and his own goal.

In diagrams 3 and 4 the four backs and the goalkeeper have a different positioning with respect to the two different positions of the opposing player with the ball.

In diagram 3.1, beside the positioning of the four backs and of the goalkeeper with respect to the position of the player with the ball, we try to explain what we mean when we say that *"the back must be placed, or in a position to get himself placed, in between the opponent and his own goal."*

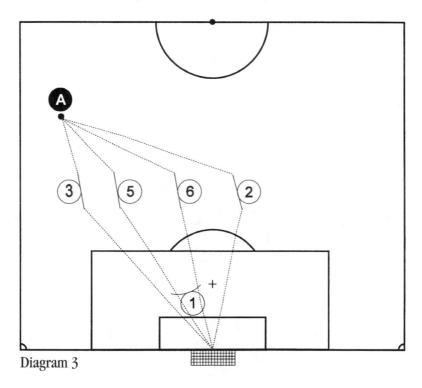

Diagram 3

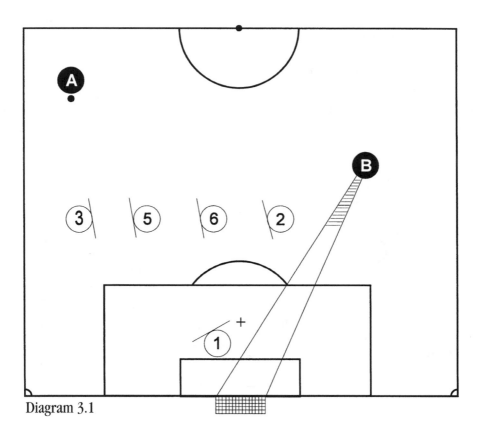

Player number 2 is positioned so that he can see the ball and his goal (just like the other backs); note he is not placed in between opposing player B and his own goal, but he is in a position to do it in case opposing player A decides to switch the direction of the play: the 3-4 seconds the ball takes to get to B enable player number 2 to "recover" his position, getting into the ideal triangle connecting the goal-line and its posts to player B. More exactly, the Right Side Back must be able to place himself into the hatched area of the triangle closer to player B.

What happens while the ball is reaching B is shown in diagram 3.2.

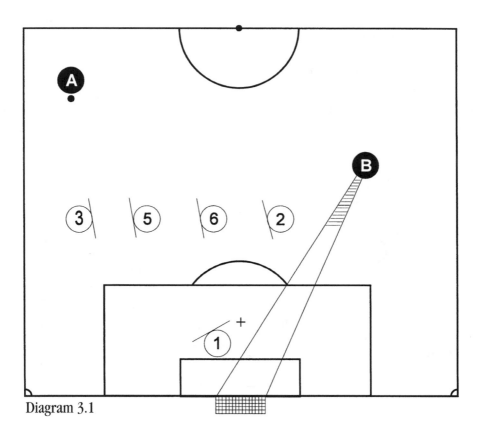

Diagram 3.1

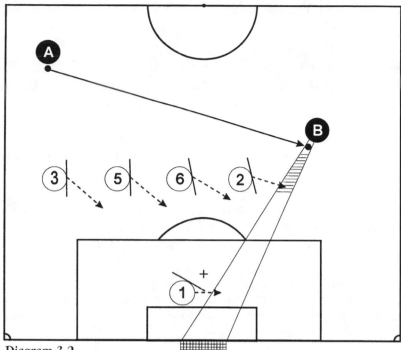

Diagram 3.2

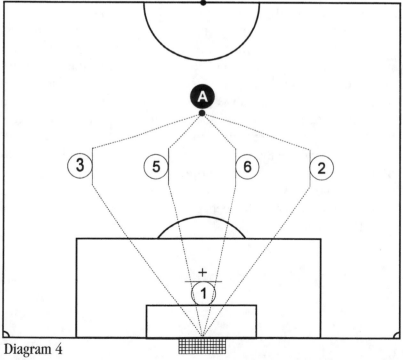

Diagram 4

# Strong Side and Weak Side

**With STRONG SIDE we mean the "side", or more generally the zone, where there is the opposing player with the ball.**

**With WEAK SIDE we mean the "side", or more generally the zone(s), away from the opposing player with the ball, where eventual opponents may be placed.**

The shorter the distance between the opponent (in the zone of a certain back) and the player with the ball, the tighter the marking that the backs playing on the strong side will have to perform, while the backs playing on the weak side will take care of covering the spaces.

*Establishing a relationship between zone marking and zone covering we can affirm that they are inversely proportional: the tighter the marking on the related opponent, the less effective the zone covering. Conversely, the more the backs cover the zone, the less tight the marking.*

In diagram 5 opposing player A with the ball is man-marked by the Left Side Back (number 3), while the Left Center Back (number 5) takes up a position to cover number 3 and is trying at the same time to mark in advance opponent B. The Right Center Back (number 6) covers number 3 and 5, while the Right Side Back (number 2) places himself along the same line as number 6, thus taking up a position to allow superiority in numbers near the zone with the opposing player with the ball. From his position, number 2 will mark in advance opponent C, trying to intercept the eventual pass or, should this not be possible, trying to stop the advance of player C if the latter gets possession of the ball through a pass from the teammate with the ball. Such a central position of the Right Side Back is not dangerous to the team if number 2 does not intercept the pass: it will take the ball 3-4 seconds to get from A to C, so if the Right Side Back (number 2) goes to cover C as soon as the ball is passed he will certainly be able to place himself between the opponent and the goal. His team-mates will then have to re-position themselves with respect to the new situation.

In diagram 6 we can see the marking inside the STRONG SIDE, while in the WEAK SIDE (the two sides) the preferred strategy is marking in advance or covering as soon as the ball is passed to one of the opponents placed there ("D"or "C"). Of course, player number 3 will see to opponent "D", while number 2 will see to "C".

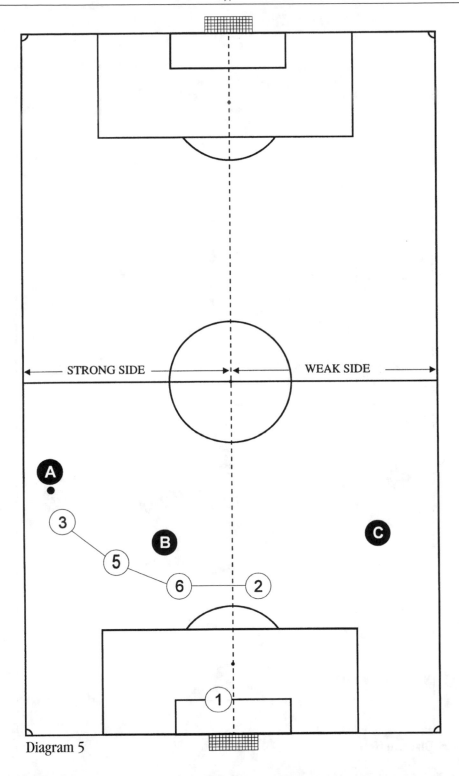

STRONG SIDE ← | → WEAK SIDE

Diagram 5

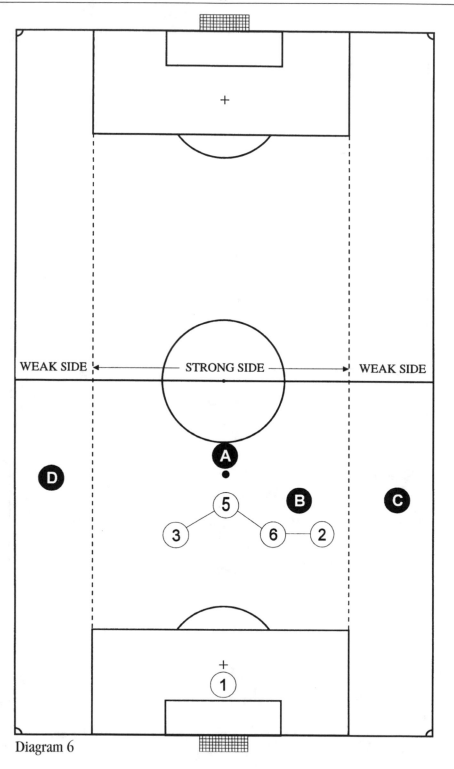

WEAK SIDE ← STRONG SIDE → WEAK SIDE

Diagram 6

## Starting Position and Attack Position

In diagram 7 we can see the 11 players arranged on the field according to what can be defined the "STARTING POSITION"; in such an arrangement, the team is ready to start a collective movement to cover the spaces with respect to the position of the ball.

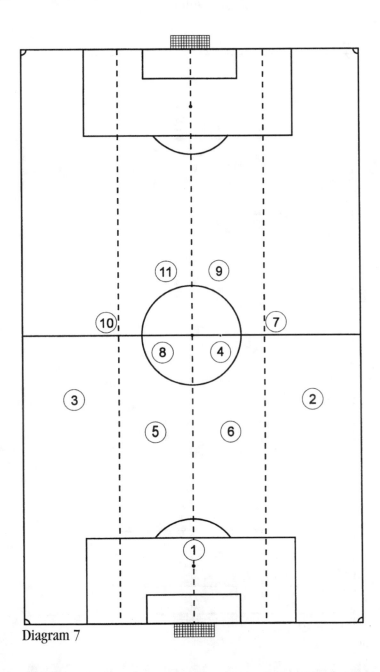

Diagram 7

In order to develop an attack, the team will have to switch from the "starting position" to a more advanced and wider one (see diagram 8), which can be defined "ATTACK POSITION".

A specific exercise based on the collective movement of the 11 players from the starting position to the attack position and vice versa could be useful to make the players familiar with the right positioning.

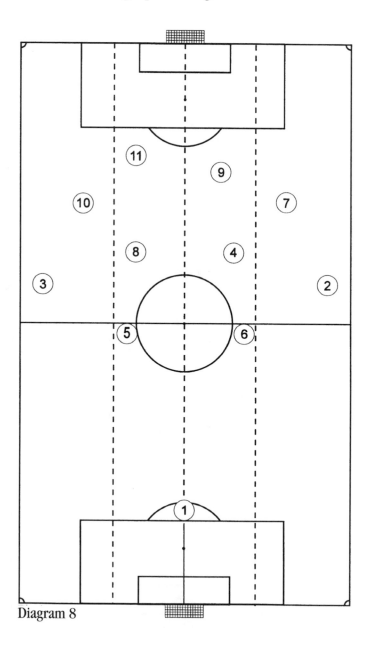

Diagram 8

While recovering the starting position, the players should run sideways so as to see both the ball in the possession of the coach (who is more advanced with respect to all the players) and their own goal.

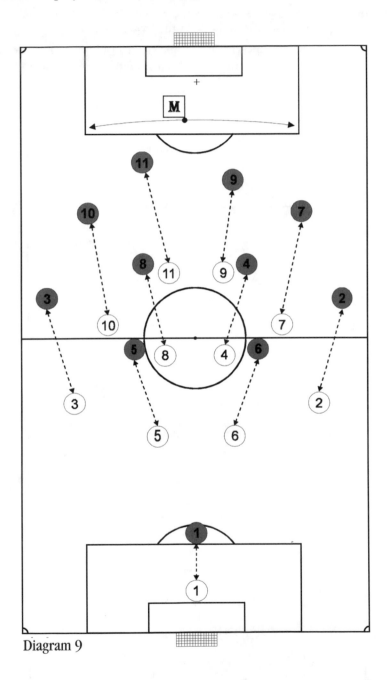

Diagram 9

# Players in Pairs and Threes

When applying a 4-4-2 pattern zone play, groups of PAIRS and THREES form almost spontaneously according to the players' position on the field.

Such clusters are necessary because the players adjacent or in nearby zones of the field must help each other thoroughly. To make it happen, the players involved in a pair or in a group of three must train in close contact so that they can get on better together and learn more about how their teammates play.

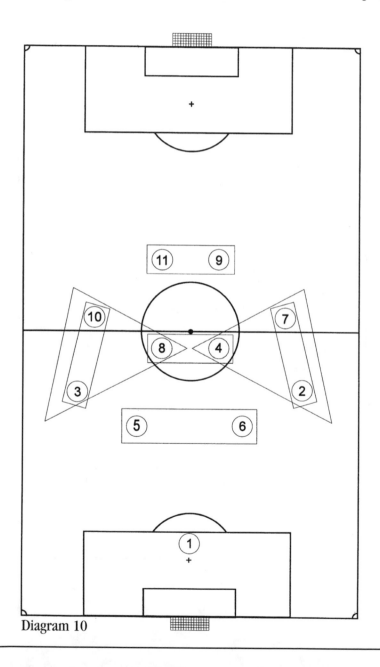

Diagram 10

Pairs and threes are pointed out in diagram 10: the related players are respectively contained in a rectangle and in a triangle.

The Left Side Back and the Left Side Midfielder are the left side pair; their collaboration is characterized by their interchange in both phases and by the good timing in double-marking on the left side (see diagrams 78-79 and 84-85).

The Right Side Back and the Right Side Midfielder are the right side pair; their collaboration is characterized by their interchange in both phases and by the good timing in double-marking on the right side.

The main characteristics that the side backs, that is the Right Side Back and the Left Side Back, should have are identical: endurance in performing breakaways along the sides at high speed, skill in cross-passing from the end of the field, effectiveness both in defending and attacking.

The main characteristics that the side midfielders, namely the Right Side Midfielder and the Left Side Midfielder should have are the same as those specified above for side backs; in addition, they should have superior basic skill and creativeness, which is fundamental in attack.

The Left Central Back and the Right Central Back are the central back pair. Besides getting on well together, they should have such skills and physical characteristics as to balance each other: speed, skill in playing with the ball off the ground, good basic skill and remarkable personality should be their main features.

The Left Central Midfielder and the Right Central Midfielder are the central midfielder pair. They too should have such characteristics as to balance each other: one of them should be physically strong, able to "tackle", good at heading; the other one, even with simple passes, should be able to give new solutions to the play. He should also be good at shooting from a distance and at making long passes. Both players should have a strong tactical sense.

The forward pair should be made up of a player able to play as a "TARGET MAN" - physically strong, good at heading and able to play with the opposing goal at his back - and by a rapid, quick forward with good individual skill, who likes starting from a distance and moving all over the attacking front.

According to this pattern we can have two threes: one on the left and one on the right. The first one is made up by the Left Side Back, the Left Side Midfielder, and the Left Central Midfielder, with all the characteristics of the players forming the pairs these three originated from. The second one is made up by the Right Side Back, the Right Side Midfielder, and the Right Central Midfielder, just like the first one, it has all the characteristics of the players forming the pairs they originated from.

In the defensive phase, the players of the three cooperate mainly by pressing the opponents playing in the advanced lateral zone (see diagrams 84-85).

When the team attacks, the players of the three cooperate mainly to start actions along the sides.

# 2

## Specific Exercises for Backs and Midfielders

*Specific Exercises on Diagonals, or Coverings, for the Back Four*

### "Static" Exercises

Four players (A-B-C-D) act as "coaches" (each of them with a ball), at such a distance as to occupy uniformly the width of the field, 15/20 yards from the line of the penalty area (diagram 11).

Each of the four backs (3-5-6-2) places himself opposite a "coach", at about 10 yards from him. When the coach gives the signal for attacking player "A" with the ball, the four backs will have to arrange themselves as shown in diagram 12, forming two lines of covering. According to such disposition, player number 5 must be in a position to cover number 3, in case the latter is beaten by "A", and to mark "B" in advance, in case "B" gets a pass from "A". Number 6 covers both number 3 and 5 and marks "C" in advance,

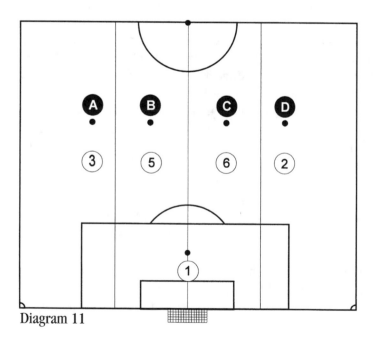

Diagram 11

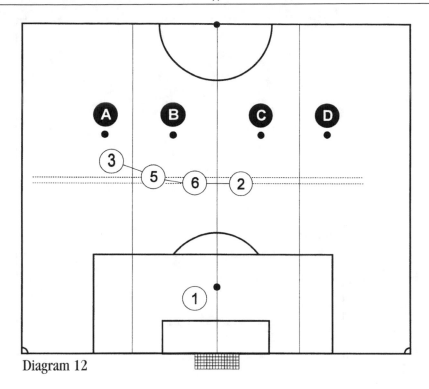

Diagram 12

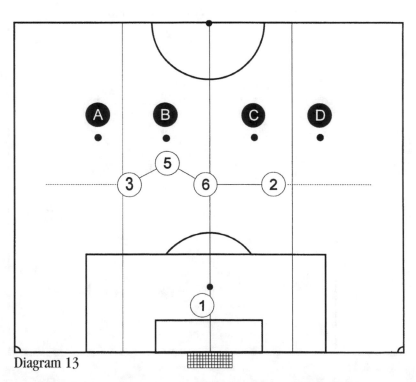

Diagram 13

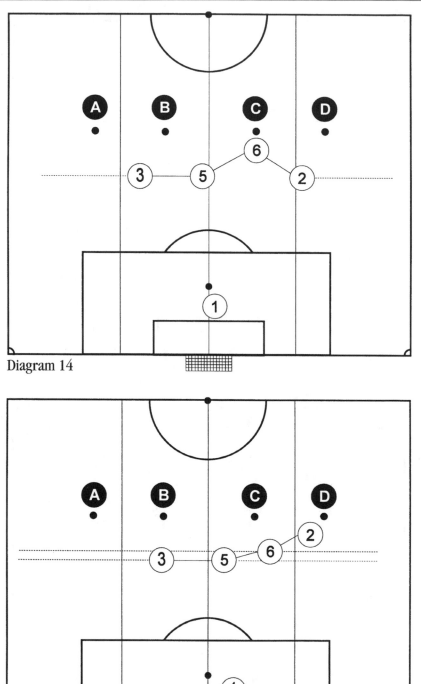

Diagram 14

Diagram 15

while number 2 will move towards the center, along the same line as number 6, so as to have superiority in numbers in the area of the man with the ball and to mark in advance or stop "D".

When the coach gives the signal, the four backs take the original arrangement again (diagram 11) and, at a new signal, they attack player "B" with the ball, placing themselves in such a way as to form only one covering line, as shown in diagram 13, in which player number 5 attacks opponent "B" with the ball, number 3 covers number 5 and at the same time marks "A" in advance, number 6 covers number 5 and marks "C" in advance, while number 2 places himself along the same line as number 3 and number 6, moving slightly towards the center in order to mark in advance or to stop "D" and to have superiority in numbers in the area of the opponent with the ball.

On the right half of the field we will have a mirroring of the tactics seen for the left half: the covering on "C" (diagram 14) will be performed as on "B", while the covering on "D" (diagram 15) will be performed as on "A".

It is important to notice that when the ball is in a lateral zone the diagonal performed has two lines of covering, pointed out by the dotted lines: by doing this, no off-side tactics will be needed, as it is difficult to apply.

When the ball is in a central zone, that is when the player with the ball is either "B" or "C", there is only one line of covering; doing this the off-side tactics become applicable almost individually, with more chances of success. If "B" is in possession of the ball (diagram 13), backs 3, 6 and 2 are along the same line, therefore, if an opponent sprints vertically, his position at the moment when the long pass is played is easily assessable by the backs. So, if when "B" plays a long pass to the forward the latter is beyond the line of the three backs, he will be off-side. However, if when the long pass is played the forward is not beyond the line of the three backs (this is not difficult to assess, as they are along the same line), they will instantly move back towards their own goal in order to stop the opponent.

When the ball is in a central zone, the goalkeeper will have to be ready to turn himself into a sweeper if the off-side trap does not work.

# Specific Exercises on Diagonals,
# or Coverings, for the Back Four

## "Dynamic" Exercises

The original arrangement of the players is shown in diagram 16. It is the same as the one seen for the "static" exercises (diagram 11), with the difference that there is only one ball which is passed from one player, acting as a "coach", to the other.

The exercise starts with "A" in possession of the ball: when the coach, with a whistle, gives the signal for attacking the player with the ball, the four backs place themselves as shown in diagram 17 (white circles), which is the same arrangement as shown in diagram 12 for the "static" exercises.

When the coach whistles again, "A" passes the ball to "B"; before "B" gets the ball, the four backs must immediately take up a new position according to the new player with the ball: such arrangement is shown in diagram 17 (shaded circles), and it is the same shown in diagram 13 for the "static" arrangement.

When the coach gives a new signal, "B" passes the ball to "C" and immediately, while the ball is still on its way to "C", the four backs take up a new position as shown in diagram 18 (white circles), which is the same as seen in diagram 14 for the "static" arrangement.

The "dynamic" sequence ends when the coach gives another signal and "C" passes the ball to "D": the backs take up the position shown in diagram 19 (shaded circles), which is the same as seen in diagram 15 for the "static" arrangement. The exercise then continues with the ball passed on in the opposite way (that is from "D" to "C", etc.) and the consequent arrangement of the four backs.

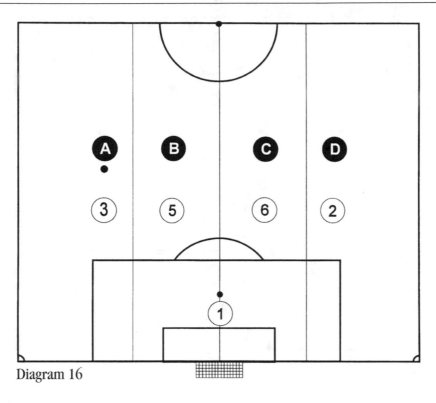

Diagram 16

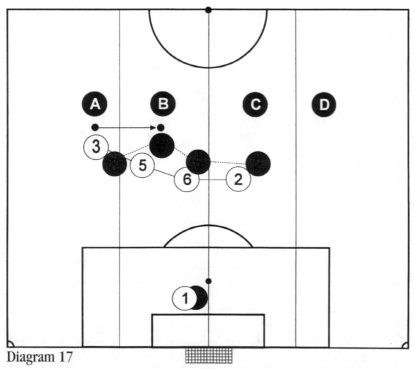

Diagram 17

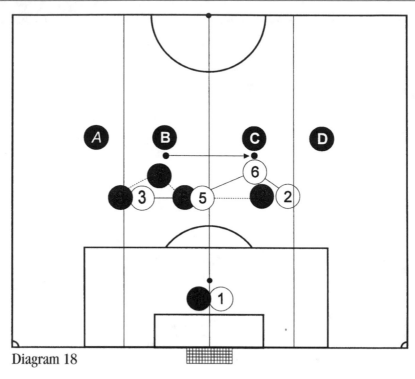

Diagram 18

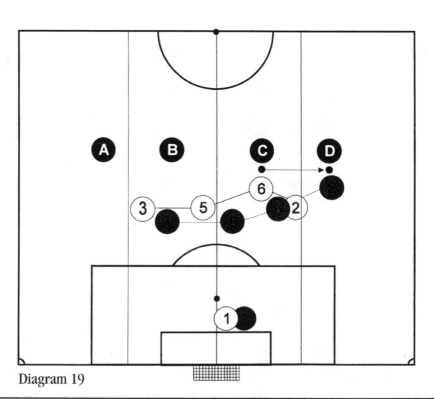

Diagram 19

# Specific Exercises on Diagonals, or Coverings, for the Four Midfielders, with Coordinated Movements of the the Back Four

## "Static" Exercises

Four players (A-B-C-D) act as "coaches" (each of them with a ball) and are placed about 5 yards beyond the midfield line in such a way as to occupy uniformly the width of the field. The four midfielders and the four backs are placed according to the "original arrangement". The two forwards do not carry out this exercise as they are not directly involved, they will be needed for double-teaming exercises.

The exercise could be performed only by the four midfielders; however, especially when training a team to the zone play for the first time, it is useful to make the backs coordinate their movements with those of the midfielders.

The exercise is carried out in the way seen for the coverings of the backs.

Diagram 20 shows the arrangement ("original arrangement" without the two forwards) to carry out the exercise.

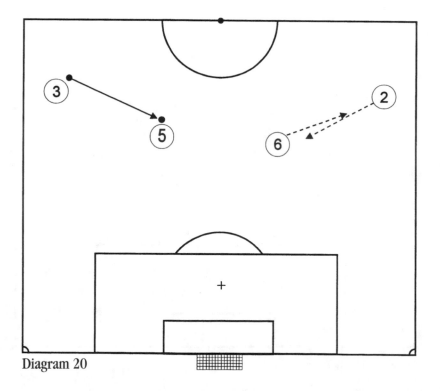

Diagram 20

When the coach gives the signal for attacking player "A" with the ball, the four midfielders and the four backs will have to place themselves as shown in picture 21; the midfield diagonal and the back diagonal are both made up of two covering lines, pointed out by the dotted lines.

The midfield diagonal enables number 8 to cover number 10 in case the latter is beaten by "A", and to mark "B" in advance. Number 4 covers both number 10 and number 8, marks in advance or stops "C" and, if needed, could double-team "B" (together with number 8). Number 7 places himself along the same line as number 4 and moves towards the center so as to have superiority in numbers in the area of the man with the ball and to mark in advance, or stop, "D".

As for the backs, when the ball is in a lateral zone they will have to form the same defensive covering (diagonal) as the midfielders.

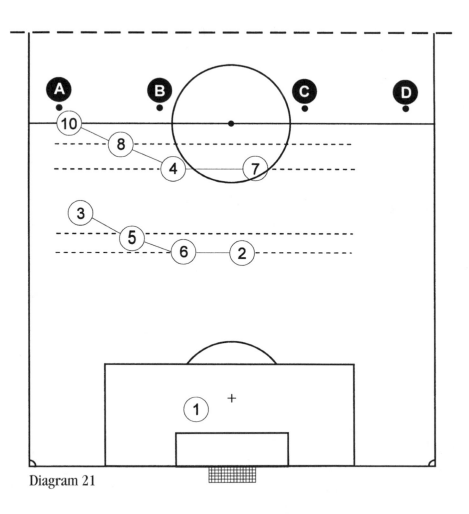

Diagram 21

When the coach gives the signal, the players take up again the original arrangement (diagram 20). Upon the next signal of the coach, the midfielders and the backs will attack player "B" with the ball and will place themselves as shown in diagram 22. Number 8 will attack player "B" with the ball, number 10 will place himself so as to cover him and to mark "A" in advance, number 4 will cover number 8 and will mark "C" in advance, while number 7 will place himself along the same line as number 4 and will move towards the center, in order to have superiority in numbers in the area of the man with the ball. If needed, number 7 could double-mark "C" (together with number 4); this position should enable him to mark in advance or to stop "D".

As the ball is in a central zone, the backs will form a "flat" covering, with the exception of one of the two central backs (number 6) standing some yards behind the others.

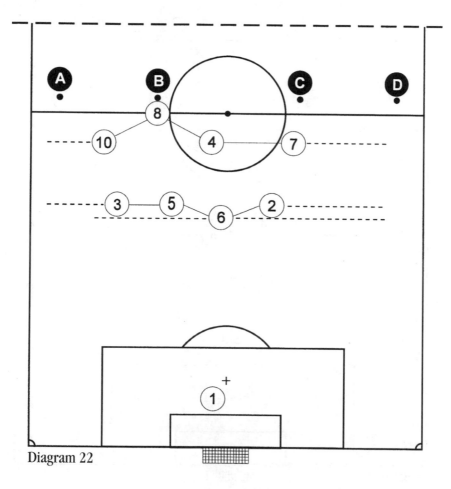

Diagram 22

The exercise continues with the players getting back to the original arrangement shown in diagram 20 and with the collective movement of attack to player "C" with the ball.

The arrangement is the one shown in diagram 23: number 4 attacks player "C" with the ball, number 7 covers number 4 and marks "D" in advance, number 8 covers number 4 and marks "B" in advance, while number 10 places himself along the same line as number 8 and moves towards the center, producing superiority in numbers in the area of the man with the ball in order to double-team "B" (together with number 8) if needed; also, such position will enable number 10 to mark in advance or stop "A".

As the ball is in a central zone, the backs will form a "flat" covering, with the exception of one of the two central backs (number 5) standing some yards behind the others.

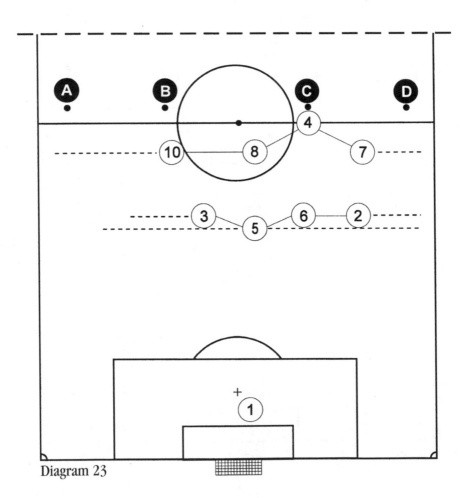

Diagram 23

The exercise continues with the players getting back to the "original arrangement" (see diagram 20) and with the attack to player "D" with the ball.

The new arrangement will be the one shown in diagram 24: number 7 attacks player "D" with the ball, number 4 covers number 7 and marks "C" in advance, number 8 covers both number 4 and number 7, marks in advance or stops "B" and, if needed, he could double-team (together with number 4) "C". Number 10 will place himself along the same line as number 8, moving towards the center so as to have superiority in numbers in the area of the man with the ball and to mark in advance, or stop, "A".

As the ball is in a lateral zone, both the midfield and the back diagonal are made up of two covering lines.

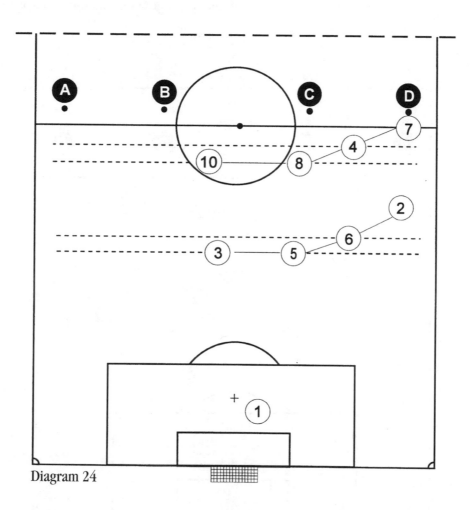

Diagram 24

# Specific Exercises on Diagonals, or Coverings, for the Four Midfielders, with Coordinated Movement of the Back Four

## "Dynamic" Exercises

The original arrangement of the players is shown in diagram 25. It is the same as the one seen for the "static" exercises (diagram 20), with the difference that there is only one ball which is passed from one player, acting as a "coach", to the other. The exercise starts with "A" in possession of the ball: when the coach, with a whistle, gives the signal for attacking the player with the ball, the four midfielders and the four backs place themselves as shown in diagram 26 (white circles), which is the same arrangement as shown in diagram 21 for the "static" exercises.

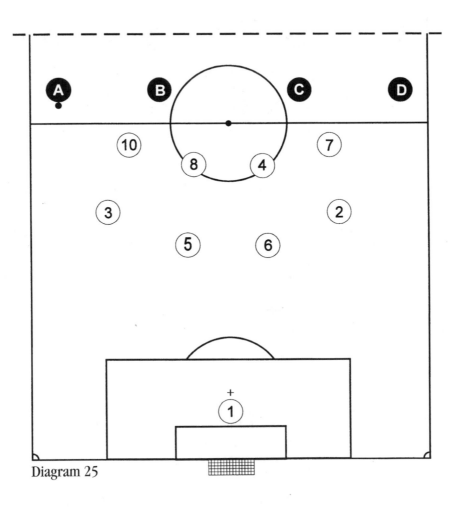

Diagram 25

When the coach whistles again, "A" passes the ball to "B"; before the latter gets the ball, the four midfielders and the four backs immediately take up the new position shown in diagram 26 (shaded circles), which is the same shown in diagram 22 for the "static" arrangement. When the coach gives a new signal, "B" passes the ball to "C" and, while the ball is still on its way to "C", the players switch from the arrangement shown in diagrams 26-27 (shaded circles) to the one shown in diagram 27 (white circles), which is the same as in diagram 23 for the "static" arrangement.

The "dynamic" sequence ends when "C" passes the ball to "D": the arrangement of the players switches from the one shown in diagrams 27-28 (white circles) to the one shown in diagram 28 (shaded circles), which is the same as in diagram 24 for the "static" exercise.

The exercise then continues with the ball passed on in the opposite way (that is from "D" to "C", etc.) and the consequent arrangement of midfielders and backs.

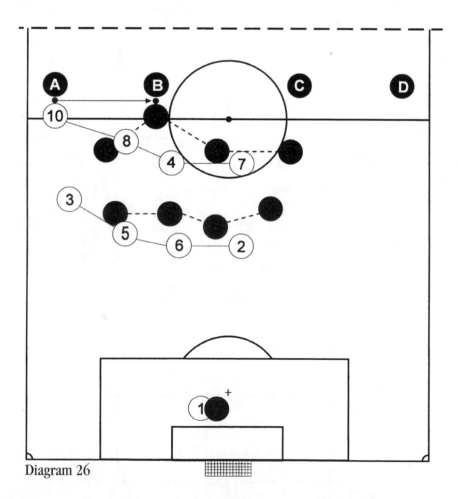

Diagram 26

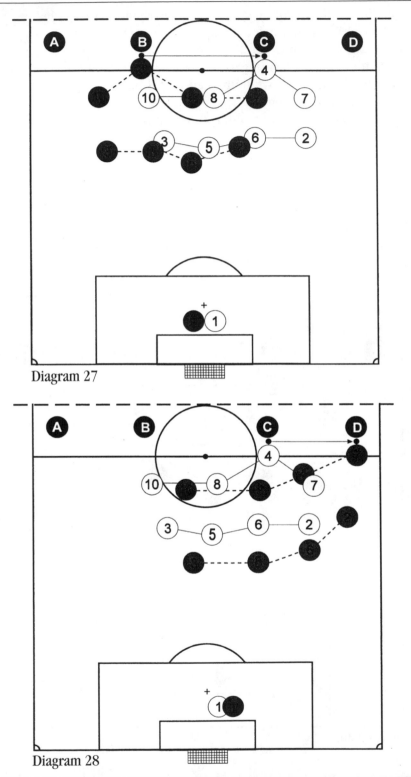

Diagram 27

Diagram 28

# Exercise Aimed at Stopping the Man with the Ball and at Marking an Overlapping Opponent Along the Left Lateral Zone, with Consequent "Updating" of the Defensive Diagonal

This exercise is shown in diagram 29: it starts with the players, midfielders and backs, in the "original arrangement" and is divided into two phases:

1. When the coach gives the first signal, the four midfielders and the back four place themselves according to player "A" with the ball, "static" in his position.

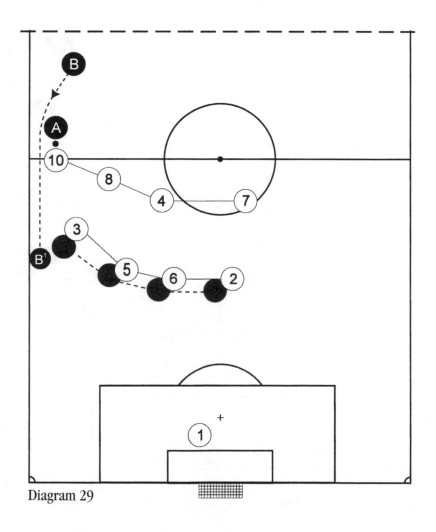

Diagram 29

2. When the coach gives the second signal, player "B", acting as a coach, overlaps "A" and places himself along the same line as the backs.

With "B" in "B1", the defensive diagonal will have to be slightly modified, so the backs will switch from the arrangement shown in diagram 29 (white circles) to the one in diagram 29 (shaded circles).

In diagram 30 there is the same exercise for the right lateral zone: the execution mirrors the one shown in diagram 29.

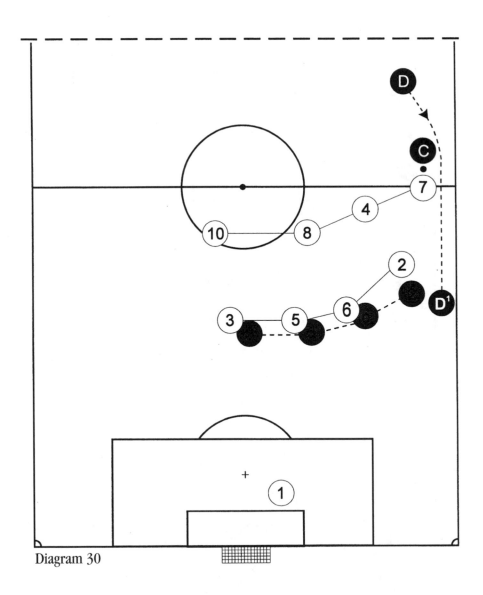

Diagram 30

# Exercises Aimed at Stopping the Man with the Ball and at Marking in Advance an Opponent Placed in the Left Lateral Zone

The exercise is shown in diagram 31: it starts with the midfielders and the backs in the "original arrangement" (white circles) and develops as follows. Player "B" is "static" in his position (in the left lateral zone) and player "A", with the ball, comes forward towards "B"; when the coach gives the signal, the midfielders and the backs must place themselves, respectively, so as to:

1. Stop player "A" with the ball, now in position "A1".

2. Mark "B" in advance.

The ensuing arrangement is shown (diagram 31) with the shaded circles.

In diagram 32 there is the same exercise for the right lateral zone: the execution mirrors the one shown in diagram 31.

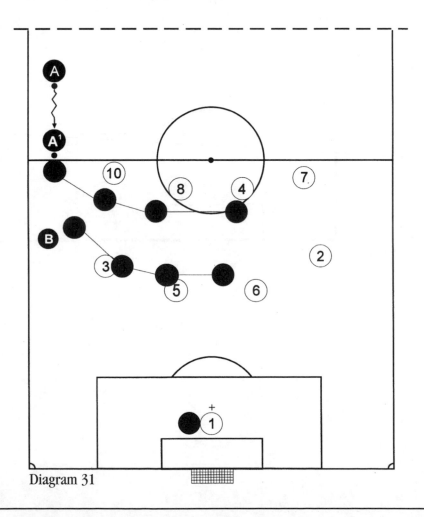

Diagram 31

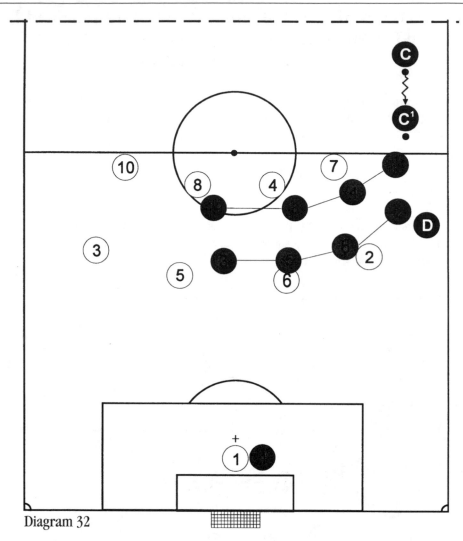

Diagram 32

# Exercise for the Two Central Backs to Interchange the Marking of an Opposing Forward When the Man with the Ball is in a Central Zone

Player "A" with the ball is "static" in his position, while "B" moves horizontally along the two central zones where the Left Central Back (number 5) and the Right Central Back (number 6) belong. The Left Central Back and the Right Central Back interchange the marking of "B", taking over when the forward gets into the respective zone where he belongs. Meanwhile, the player not directly involved in the marking of "B" will cover his teammate.

Diagrams 33-34-35-36 show four different positions of the forward, with the related arrangement of the two central backs.

When training a team for the zone play for the first time, the marking of the opposing forward should be interchanged verbally. When the understanding between the two backs increases, they will stop "switching" verbally the marking of the opponent: a simple sign will be enough.

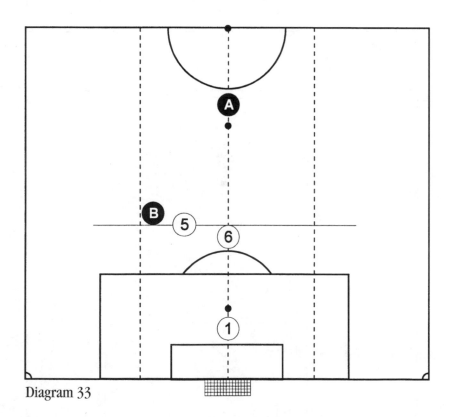

Diagram 33

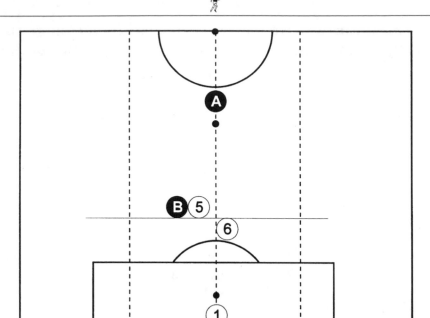

Diagram 34

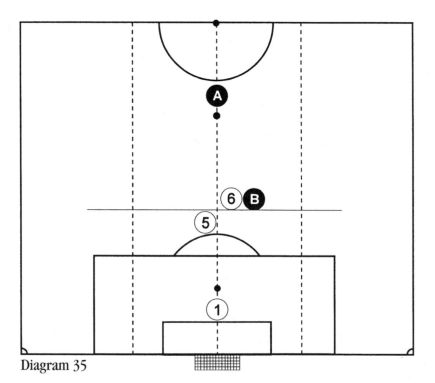

Diagram 35

# Exercise for the Back Four to Interchange the Marking of an Opposing Forward when the Man with the Ball is in a Central Zone

Player "A" with the ball is "static" in his position, while opponent "B" moves horizontally along the attack front.

The four backs take turns at marking "B", each of them taking over when the forward gets into the respective zone where he belongs. One of the two central backs (depending on the position of the forward) will cover his teammate involved in the marking.

Diagrams 37-38-39-40 show four different positions of forward "B", with the related arrangement of the four backs.

If "B" moves towards the lateral zones (weak side) the side backs will follow him up to a certain point, after which they will mark him in advance.

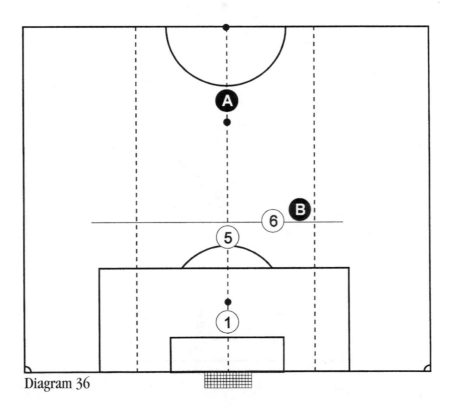

Diagram 36

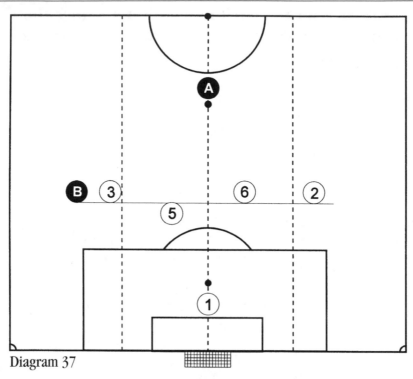

Diagram 37

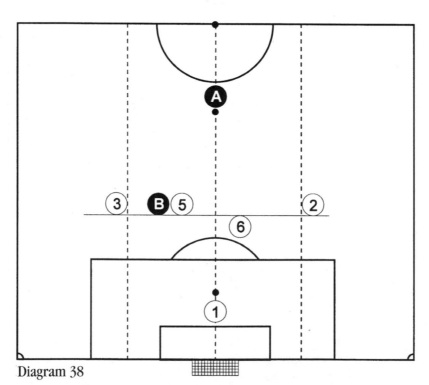

Diagram 38

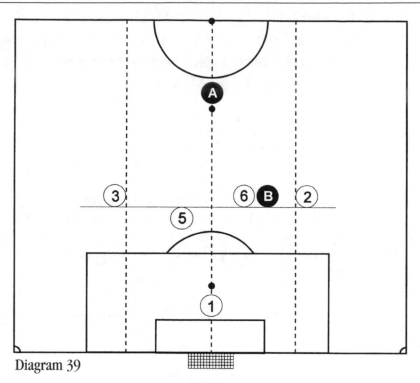

Diagram 39

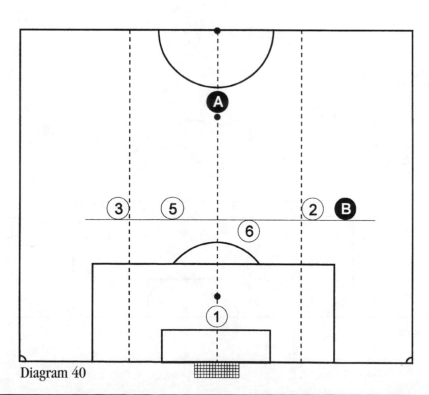

Diagram 40

# Exercise for the Back Four to Interchange the Marking of an Opposing Forward when the Man with the Ball is in the Left Lateral Zone and Arrangement of the Four Midfielders

The exercise starts with the midfielders and the backs in the "original arrangement"; player "A" with the ball is "static" in his position, as well as forward "B" (diagram 41).

When the coach gives the signal, the midfielders form a covering line on player "A" with the ball and the backs place themselves with respect to the position of the man with the ball and mark forward "B".

In diagram 41, "B" is marked by the Left Side Back (number 3) as the forward is in the zone where he belongs.

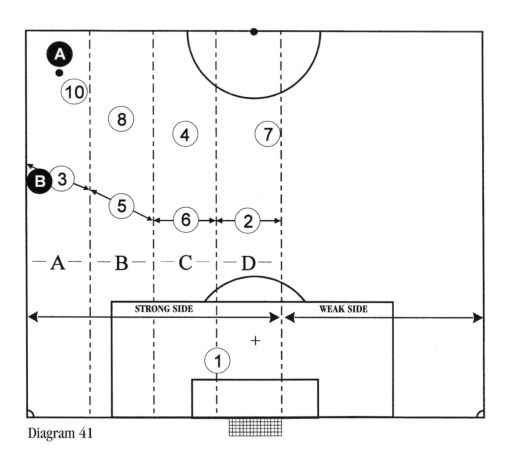

Diagram 41

The exercise continues with "B" moving along all the attack front, with the ensuing interchange of the marking by the backs according to the zone the forward occupies.

When "B" enters the so-called "weak side" (diagram 45) the Right Side Back (number 2) does not follow him, but he marks him in advance; therefore, when the forward is in "B1" position, the position of number 2 is almost the same.

The different arrangements of the backs with respect to the different position of forward "B" can be found in diagrams 42-43-44-45.

The exercise is carried out with the man with the ball in the left lateral zone. The exercise with the man with the ball in the right lateral zone is not illustrated as its execution simply mirrors the one we have just described.

In diagram 41 we can notice how, in consideration of what has already been said about the weak side and the strong side, the zones watched by each single back become smaller, depending on the position of the ball, if compared to the purely theoretical ones seen in diagram 4.

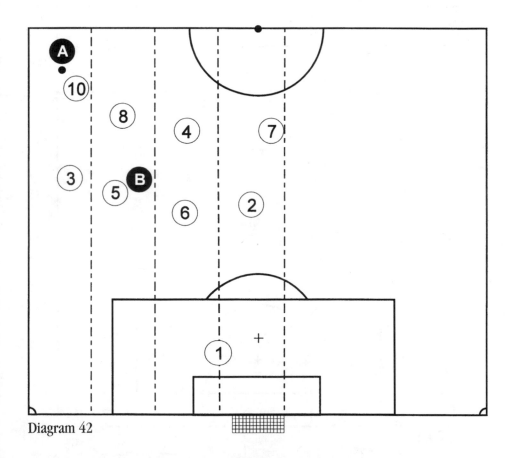

Diagram 42

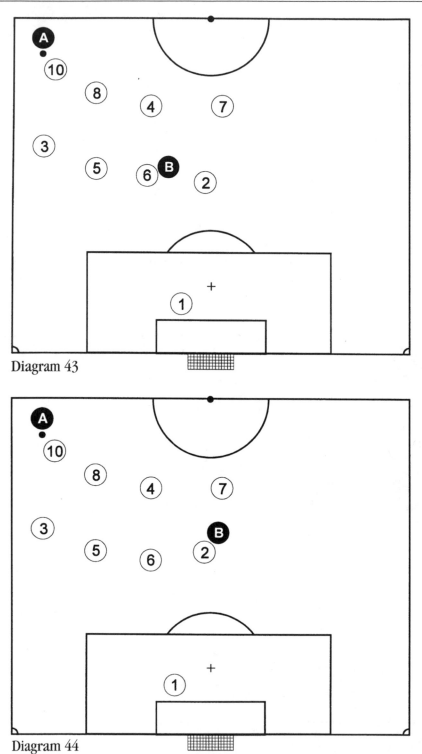

Diagram 43

Diagram 44

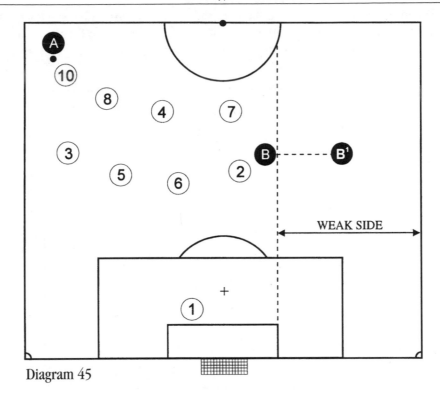

Diagram 45

WEAK SIDE

## Exercise for the Back Four to Interchange the Marking of Two Opposing Forwards when the Man with the Ball is in the Left Lateral Zone and Arrangement of the Midfielders

The exercise starts with the midfielders and the backs in the "original arrangement"; player "A" with the ball is "static" in his position, and the forwards "B" and "C" are also "static" in the position shown in diagram 46.

When the coach gives the signal, the midfielders form the covering line on player "A" with the ball and the backs place themselves with respect to the position of the man with the ball and mark the two forwards as shown in diagram 46.

The exercise continues with the forwards moving along all the attack front, with the ensuing interchange of the marking by the backs according to the zone the forwards occupy.

The different arrangements of the backs with respect to the different position of forwards "B" and "C" can be found in diagrams 47-48-49-50-51.

When possible, it is better to have a "safety" man (temporary sweeper); only in the case shown in diagram 50, given the arrangement of the forwards, it is not possible to place a man behind the line of the marking players.

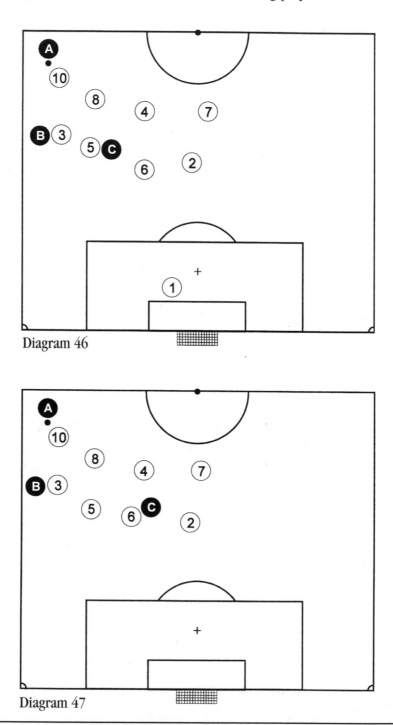

Diagram 46

Diagram 47

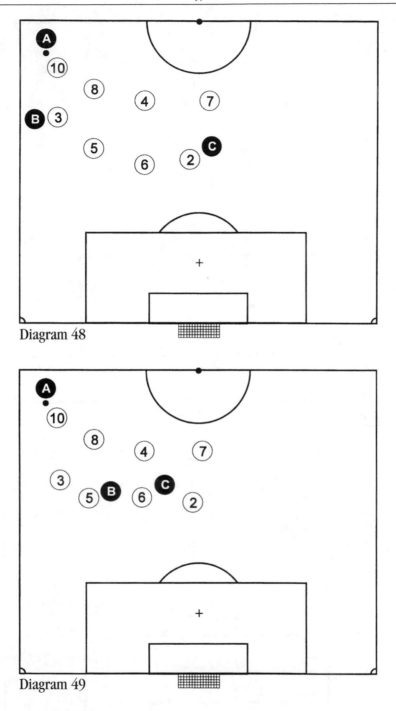

Diagram 48

Diagram 49

The exercise is carried out with the man with the ball in the left lateral zone. The exercise with the man with the ball in the right lateral zone is not illustrated as its execution simply mirrors the one we have just described.

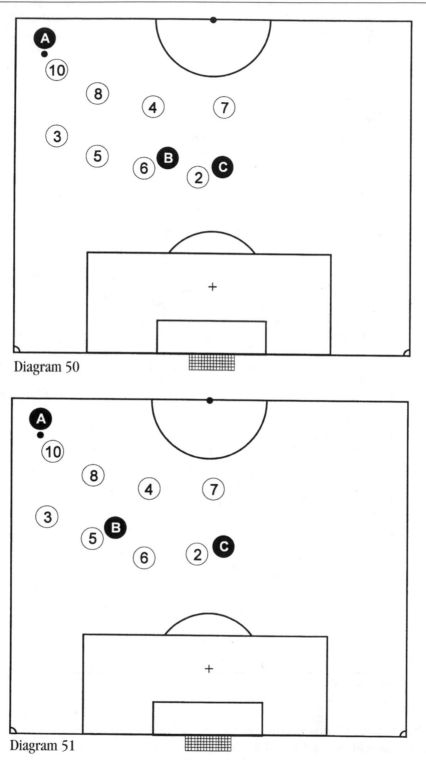

Diagram 50

Diagram 51

# Exercise for the Back Four to Interchange the Marking of an Opposing Forward when the Man with the Ball is in the Center-Left Zone of the Midfield and Arrangement of the Four Midfielders

The exercise starts with the midfielders and the backs in the "original arrangement"; player "A" with the ball is "static" in his position, as well as forward "B" (diagram 52).

When the coach gives the signal, the midfielders form the covering line on player "A" with the ball and the backs place themselves with respect to the position of the man with the ball and mark forward "B".

In diagram 52, "B" is marked by the Left Side Back (number 3) as the forward is in the zone where he belongs.

The exercise continues with "B" moving along all the attack front, with the ensuing interchange of the marking by the backs according to the zone the forward occupies. When "B" enters the so-called "weak side" zones, number 2 (see diagram 56) and number 3 (see diagram 57) do not follow him, but mark him in advance.

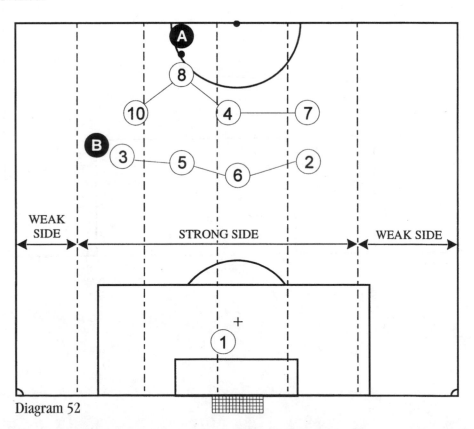

Diagram 52

In diagrams 56 and 57 we can notice that the advance of number 2 on forward "B" is more marked if compared to the advance of number 3 on "B", because in the first case the distance between the forward and his teammate in possession of the ball is bigger than in the second case.

The different arrangements of the backs with respect to the different position of forward "B" can also be found in diagrams 53-54-55.

The exercise is carried out with the man with the ball in the center-left zone of the midfield. The exercise with the man with the ball in the center-right zone of the midfield is not illustrated as its execution simply mirrors the one we have just described.

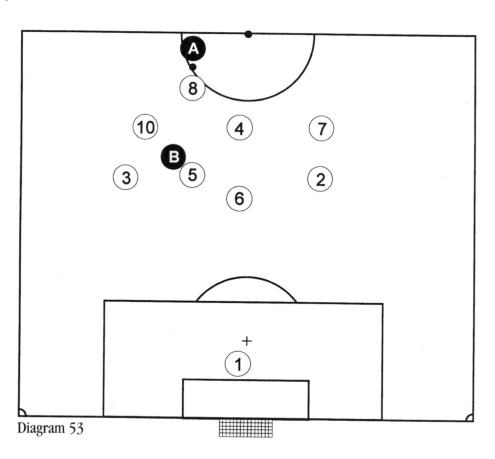

Diagram 53

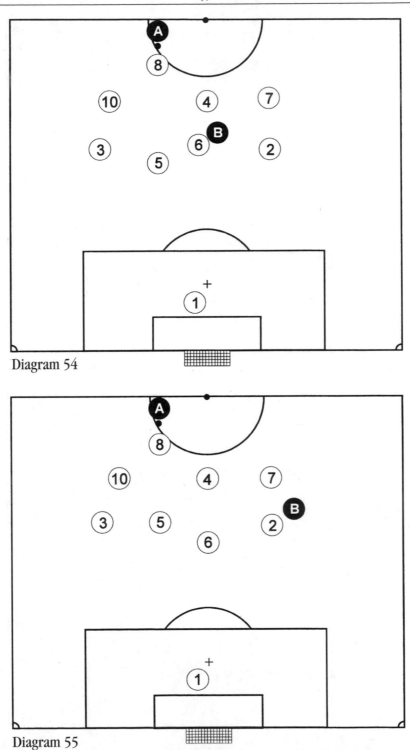

Diagram 54

Diagram 55

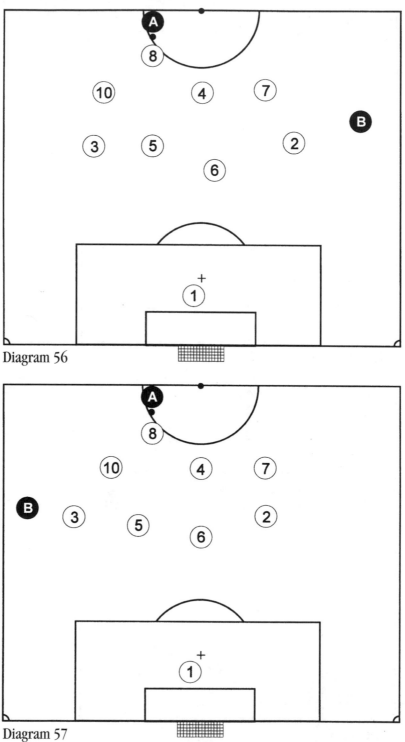

Diagram 56

Diagram 57

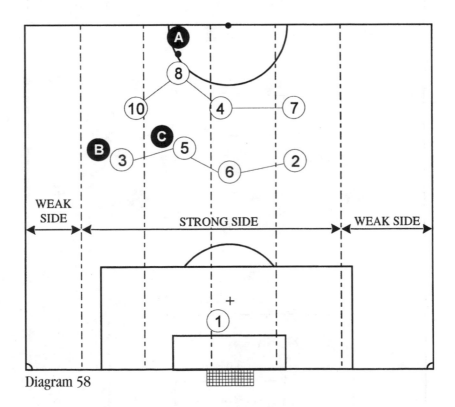

# Exercise for the Back Four to Interchange the Marking of Two Opposing Forwards when the Man with the Ball is in the Center-Left Zone of the Midfield and Arrangement of the Four Midfielders

The exercise starts with the midfielders and the backs in the "original arrangement"; player "A" with the ball is "static" in his position, and the forwards "B" and "C" are also "static" in the position shown in diagram 58.

When the coach gives the signal, the midfielders form the covering line on player "A" with the ball and the backs place themselves with respect to the position of the man with the ball and mark the two forwards as shown in diagram 58.

The exercise continues with "B" and "C" moving along all the attack front, with the ensuing interchange of the marking by the backs according to the position of the forwards.

The different arrangements of the backs with respect to the different position of forwards "B" and "C" can be found in diagrams 59-60-61-62-63.

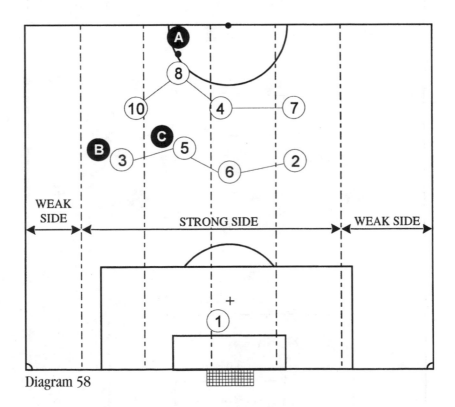

Diagram 58

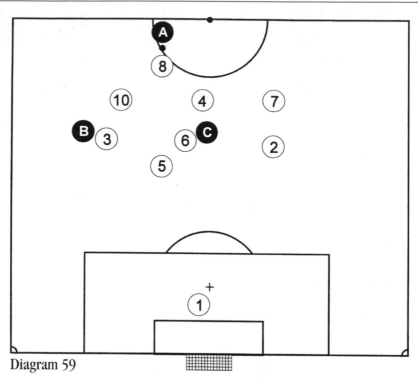

Diagram 59

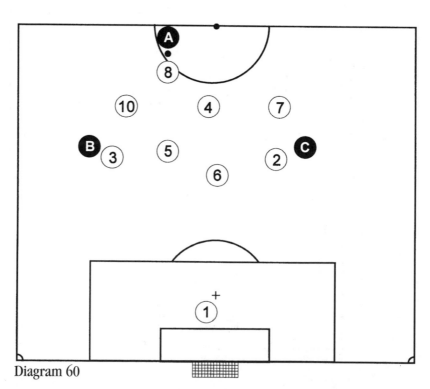

Diagram 60

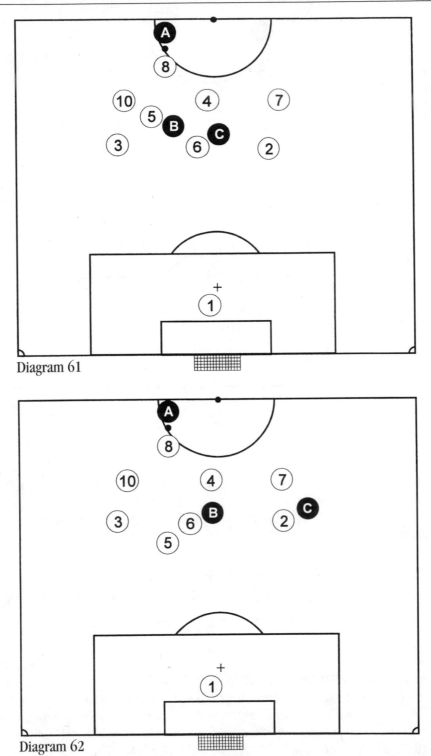

Diagram 61

Diagram 62

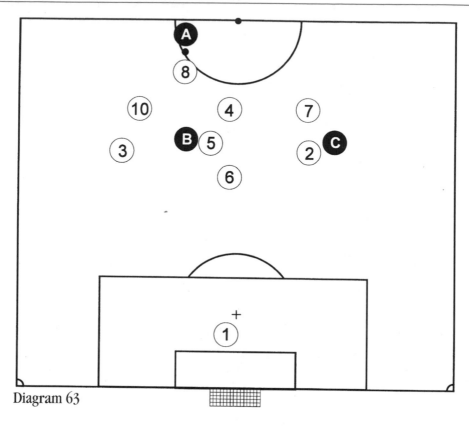

Diagram 63

The exercise is carried out with the man with the ball in the center-left zone of the midfield. The exercise with the man with the ball in the center-right zone of the midfield is not illustrated as its execution simply mirrors the one we have just described.

## Global Exercises for Midfielders and Backs, Aiming at Forming the Midfield Diagonal and at Marking the Two Opposing Forwards

Four players (A-B-C-D) act as "coaches" and, placed as shown in diagram 64, pass the ball to each other from the right to the left and vice versa.

The exercise starts with midfielders and backs in the "original arrangement", with player "A" in possession of the ball and the two forwards "E" and "F" who place themselves, for example, as shown in diagram 64.

When the coach gives the signal, the midfielders place themselves according to the position of player "A" with the ball and the backs do the same thing, marking the two forwards. After that, the ball is passed from "A" to "B", from "B" to "C", from "C" to "D", from "D" to "C", from "C" to "B" etc., and forwards "E" and "F" move freely all over the attack front (see diagram 65). In this way the midfielders place themselves according to the position of the ball: they form the midfield covering or diagonal, and the backs, besides placing themselves according to the position of the ball, will have to "take turns" at marking the two forwards, following the principles seen in the previous pages.

The coach can interrupt the exercise, making all the players stay where they are, in order to modify the midfield covering and, above all, the defensive covering, or to confirm the correctness of the arrangement.

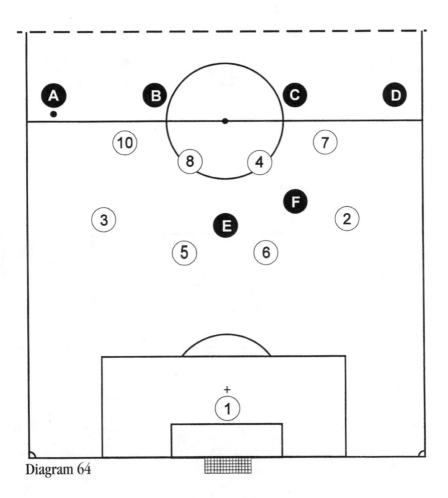

Diagram 64

In a second phase, once the exercises previously explained have been assimilated, the same exercise can be performed with three forwards (instead of two) moving freely all over the attacking front.

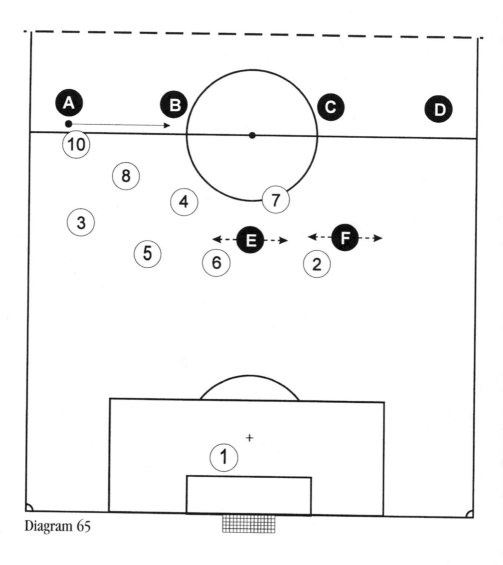

Diagram 65

# 3

# Strategy, Tactics, Short and Tight Team, Pressure and Off-Side

## Definition of Strategy

A strategy is a game plan through which, bearing in mind the rules of the game, one's own strong and weak points, the possible behavior of the opponent(s), and the expected match conditions, the potential decisions on the way the team will play during the match are mentally anticipated and established.

## Definition of Tactics

Tactics are all the different ways the team may play, the actions and the individual and collective operations of the players through which, bearing in mind the rules of the game, the actions of one's own teammates and of the opponents, as well as the eventual external factors and conditions, may be influenced and used to one's own advantage.

## Connection Between Strategy and Tactics

While strategy, in planning the behavior, bears in mind the possibilities of decision of the opponent(s) but does not influence them, tactics refers to the targeted use of actions paving the way for the realization of the strategy. Tactics aim at conditioning situations of play and opponents through misleading choices that will have an impact on one's own and the opponent's behavior, and it comprises the necessary knowledge and skills.

## Short and Tight Team

In modern play as a whole, and in zone play in particular, when the ball is in the opponent's possession the team must arrange itself on the field in such a way as to be SHORT (with respect to the length of the field, all the players should be placed in about 30 yards) and TIGHT (with respect to the width of the field, the players will place themselves so as to have superiority in numbers in the zone where the ball is).

In order to explain the concept of "tight team" we must refer to what we said about the "strong side" and the "weak side" (diagrams 5 and 6). When the team attacks it must still be SHORT, even with changes in the positions of the players (who will arrange themselves according to the "attack position", diagram 8), but it must not be TIGHT any more; it must try to take as many players as possible beyond the line of the ball, placed in such a way as to allow the player with the ball different solutions and options of play. The players should also be at a distance from the player with the ball that enables them to be reached through a (long)pass. Another aim linked to the arrangement of the players (again, when attacking) is to try to make the distances between the opponents get bigger, so as to have wider spaces to develop the action.

## Pressure

Pressure can be defined as the team movement that closes the space on the man with the ball, reducing his available time of play.

Pressure is the coordinated movement of several players aiming at forcing the man with the ball to perform a predictable move (dribble or pass) or a chance move, enabling them to regain possession of the ball.

Pressure can be applied starting from three different positions:

a) from the limit of the opposing penalty area;

b) from the limit of the attack third of the field;

c) from the midfield line.

The position where a team starts to apply pressure from depends basically on three factors:

1) the characteristics of the two forwards;

2) the physical condition of the players;

3) the presumed strength of the opposing team.

Of course, the application of pressure can be modified during the match according to its outcome.

If the two forwards are particularly fast (that is if their characteristics are ideal for counterattack), pressure should be started from the midfield line.

Conversely, if the two forwards are not particularly fast but are characterized by other skills (for example, if they are opportunists and good at heading) pressure should be started from the limit of the attacking third of the field or even beyond.

As for the relationship between the "strength of the opposing team and the position to start pressure from,"

a) if the opposing team is weaker, pressure should be started from the limit of the opposing area;

b) if the opposing team is of equal calibre, pressure should be started from the opposing limit of the attacking third of the field;

c) if the opposing team is potentially stronger, the two forwards should return to your midfield and pressure should be started from the midfield line.

The application of pressure in a certain area or position also depends on the

## Off-Side Tactics

In the general strategy of the team, the off-side tactics could be defined as all those actions aiming at regaining possession of the ball, which can take place in two specific ways:

a) by receiving an indirect free kick;
b) taking the ball away from the opponents thanks to the application of pressure.

If we opt for the application of the off-side tactics, the simultaneous application of pressure is absolutely essential, except if we want to apply it on the occasion of free kicks as shown in diagrams 92 and 92.1.

In respect to the application of the off-side tactics, the following situations will be taken into account:

1) defensive equality or inferiority in numbers (examples shown in diagrams 71-72-73 and 74-75-76-77) ;
2) clearance in central area after a long or cross pass(example shown in diagrams 89-89.1);
3) clearance in central area after a corner kick (similar to example in diagrams 89-89.1);
4) when the forward makes a back pass with the goal at his back (example shown in diagrams 93-93.1-93.2-93.3);

When applying an off-side trap, one of the two central backs must "lead" the off-side, calling the time of its execution even with a password.

The choice between the two backs will be previously made by the coach according to their skills.

As we have already said, the off-side tactics need a simultaneous application of pressure; to leave the opponents off-side without applying pressure on the player with the ball would mean to "invite" the latter to perform a single action, with a high chance of success.

Instead, pressure can be applied without having to resort to off-side.

In this book we will not give examples of specific situations in which off-side could be applied with a forward sprint by the backs at the moment when the opposing player with the ball makes a long pass towards his forwards.

On such specific situations, the application of the off-side trap is similar to the one on free kicks. It is as if the long pass from "B" (diagrams 92 and 92.1) does not take place when the ball is still but during open play.

As for the application of the off-side trap on a long vertical pass starting from a central area, see note 2.

The application of the off-side trap on long passes to the forwards and on deep passes is important, but if it is done systematically it can, sooner or later, be vulnerable to mistakes and give the opposing team a chance to take countermeasures more than the application of the off-side trap in the situations listed above (points 1-2-3-4).

# 4

# Situations of Superiority, Equality and Inferiority in Numbers in the Defensive Phase

**Situation: 2 v 3 (defensive superiority in numbers)**

In diagram 66 we can see an action by the opponents who are inferior in numbers with respect to your backs (2 forwards against 3 backs).

After regaining possession of the ball in the midfield third of the field, forward "A" runs towards your area; at the same time, his teammate "B" cuts horizontally. In diagram 66 we can see that, while "A" attacks, the Left Central Back (number 5) faces him thus playing for time and the Right Central Back (number 6) and the Right Side Back (number 2) move backward. At the same time, "B" cuts from the center towards the left, being marked first by the Right Side Back (number 2) and then by the Right Central Back (number 6), who marks him up to the extreme left, as the Left Central Back (number 5) is already marking the player with the ball. The way in which the defensive situation evolves is shown starting from diagram 66 through diagram 67 and finally in diagram 68.

In the new situation shown in diagram 68, player number 2 covers number 5 and, as we have already said, number 6 marks forward "B".

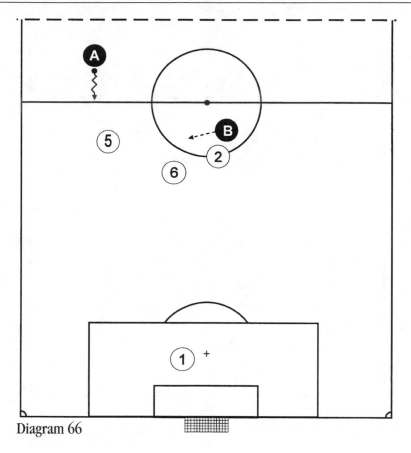

Diagram 66

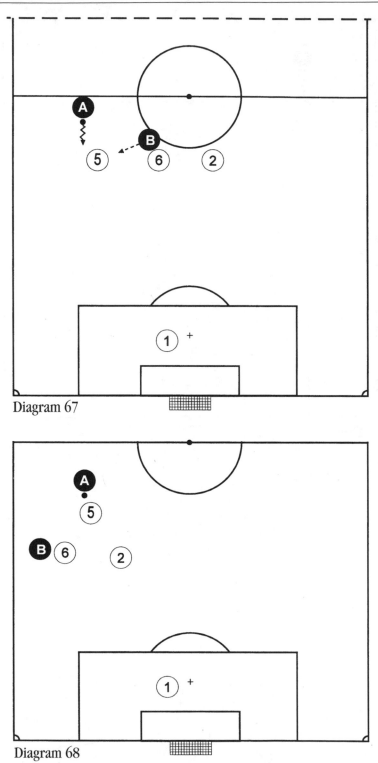

Diagram 67

Diagram 68

## Situation: 3 v 4 (defensive superiority in numbers)

In diagram 69 we can see an attack by 3 players (A-B-C), while the defending team (ours) has 4 players in the right position to intercept.

Opponent "A" moves quickly forward with the ball in a central position, supported by "B" and "C".

The backs immediately place themselves as shown in diagram 70: the Left Central Back (number 5) attacks the player with the ball, the Right Side Back (number 2) marks "C", the Left Side Back (number 3) marks "B" and the Right Central Back (number 6) covers number 5, placing himself temporarily as a sweeper, without getting too far from his three teammates.

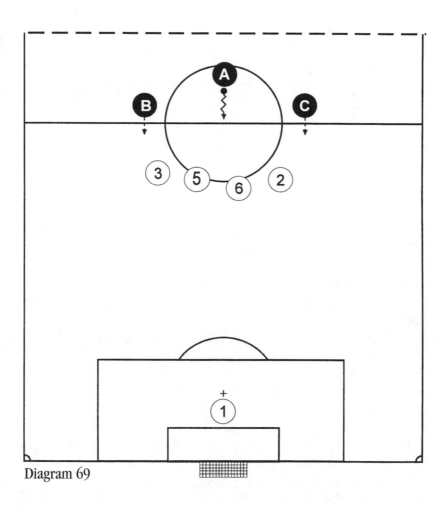

Diagram 69

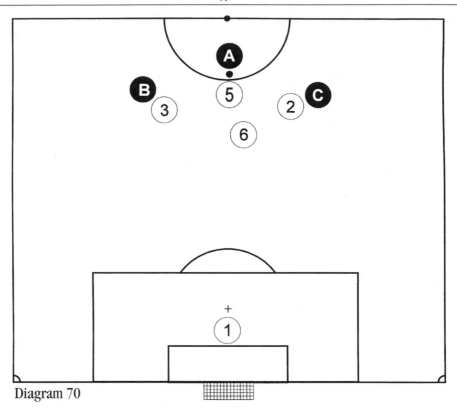

Diagram 70

## Situation: 3 v 3 (equality in numbers)

### *Application of the Off-Side Tactics*

Diagram 71 shows a counterattack by the opponents in conditions of equality in numbers.

Player "A" moves quickly forward with the ball, supported by forwards "B" and "C".

There is equality in numbers and the team applies the off-side tactics which we exemplify; however, in such situations other options are possible. The offside tactics are applied in conditions of inferiority in numbers and it could be applied also in conditions of equality in numbers. In the situation shown, we have wanted to give an example of the application of the offside trap in conditions of equality in numbers, but other forms of interdiction could be possible.

In diagram 72 the three backs (number 5, 6 and 2) step backwards, biding their time to apply pressure on the player with the ball and to apply the off-side trap. Number 6 faces the player with the ball and plays for time, so as to seize the right moment to attack "A" supported by the other two backs (number 2 and 5) who place themselves along the same line with the forward further back ("B" in diagram 72).

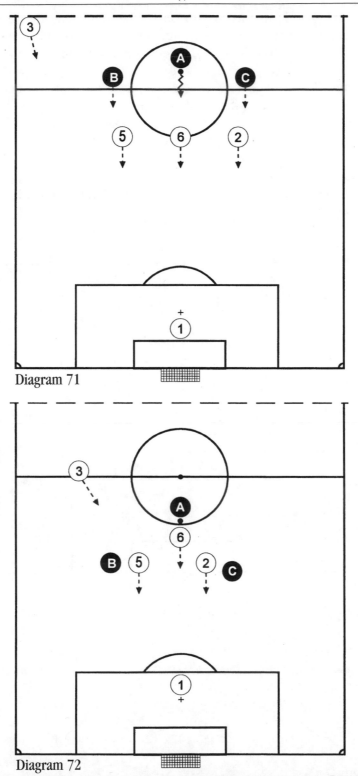

Diagram 71

Diagram 72

Playing for time is important, not only when choosing the right time to attack, but also in order to give one's teammates the time to return. For example, even if we have a 3 v 3 situation, we showed a returning back (number 3) in diagram 72.

In diagram 73, when number 6 attacks the player with the ball number 5 and 2 move immediately forward, thus triple-teaming "A" and leaving "B" and "C" off-side if either of them should receive a pass from "A". Given the resulting superiority in numbers (3 v 1), if "A" decides to dribble and not to pass the ball, the three backs have good chances of seizing the ball.

In the application of the off-side trap the goalkeeper is extremely important: he must be ready to get out of his penalty area and stop the attack if the off-side trap does not work.

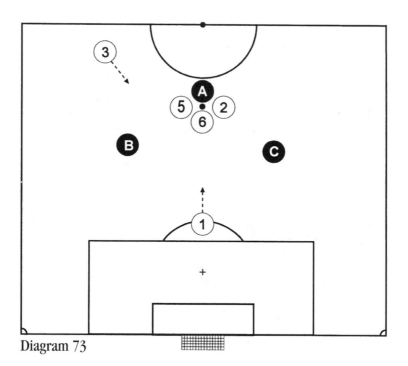

Diagram 73

## Situation: 3 v 2 (defensive inferiority in numbers)

### *Application of the Off-Side Trap*

Diagram 74 shows a counterattack by the opponents in conditions of inferiority in numbers.

Player "A" moves quickly forward with the ball, supported by forwards "B" and "C".

Given the inferiority in numbers, the team applies the off-side trap as shown in the example.

From diagram 74 to 75, we can see that number 5 and 6 play for time and at the same time shorten their distance from the player with the ball. Besides

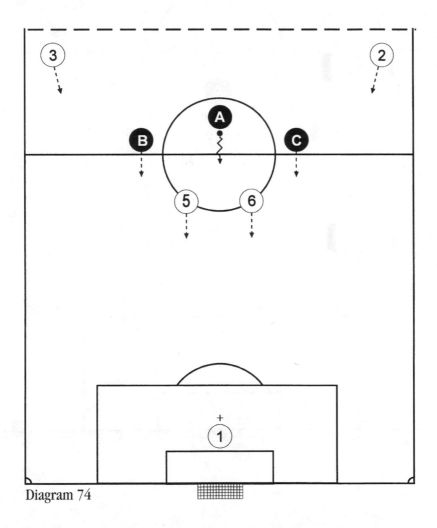

Diagram 74

giving other teammates (in this case, number 2 and 3) the time to return, the two central backs aim at placing themselves along the same line as the trailing forward (in diagram 76 it is forward "B"); as soon as they are along the same line, the two backs apply the off-side trap and at the same time apply pressure on "A" (see diagram 76).

Diagram 77 shows the situation resulting from pressure aiming at leaving the opponents off-side. It should be noticed that when the two central backs apply the off-side trap the goalkeeper is ready to get out of his penalty area.

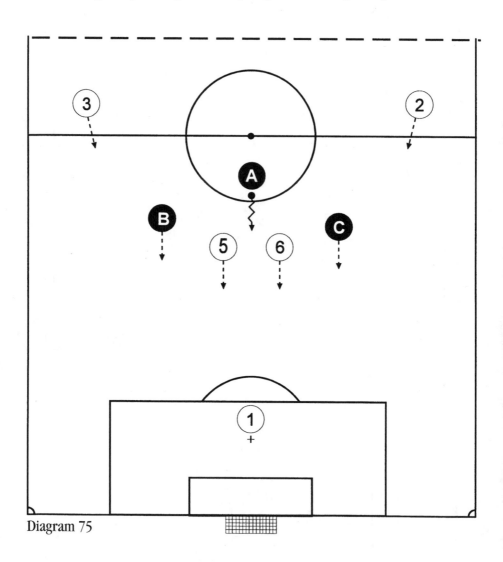

Diagram 75

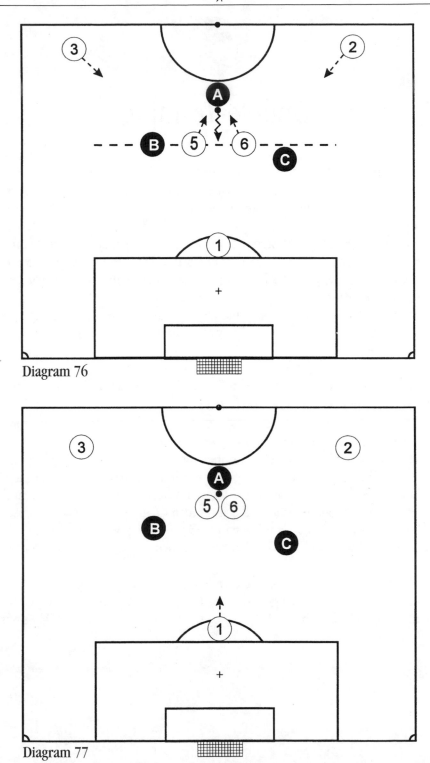

Diagram 76

Diagram 77

# 5

# Double-Teaming

## Double-Teaming on Various Zones of the Field, Group Exercises

In order to make such exercises seem real we will simulate situations as close to reality as possible, pretending we are facing a team playing according to a 5-3-2 pattern.

Of course, when playing against a team arranged according to a different pattern the situations will be different, but starting from the situation we propose it will be easy for the coach to make slight adjustments in order to arrange double-teaming according to the different pattern of the team to face.

Our aim is to make clear the principle through which double-teaming must be carried out: this principle will always be valid, no matter how the opposing team is arranged.

## Double-teaming in the Midfield left side Zone, Carried out by the Left Side Midfielder and the Left Side Back

Diagram 78 shows a hypothetical opposing team, arranged according to a 5-3-2 pattern, for the purpose of training your team.

The exercise starts with the five opposing backs (A-B-C-D-E) who pass the ball between themselves from the right to the left and from the left to the right. While they do so, all the players of the team apply pressure; this means that when the ball is in possession of the three central players (B-C-D) forwards 9 and 11 will apply pressure, while when it is in "A's" possession number 7 will attack him; finally, when "E" is in possession of the ball, number 10 will attack him.

Let's analyze the situation at the moment when the ball goes from "C" to "D": all the players will change their position according to the new position of the ball; they will place themselves as shown in diagram 78, as "D" is in possession of the ball.

Then, "D" passes the ball to "E" (diagram 79); double-teaming must be carried out during the time the ball takes to get from "D" to "E".

As diagram 79 shows, number 10 and 3 double-team while number 11 marks the back pass, number 9 marks the pass to the center, number 5 covers number 3 and all the others mark in advance the closest attacker. Number 7, besides being

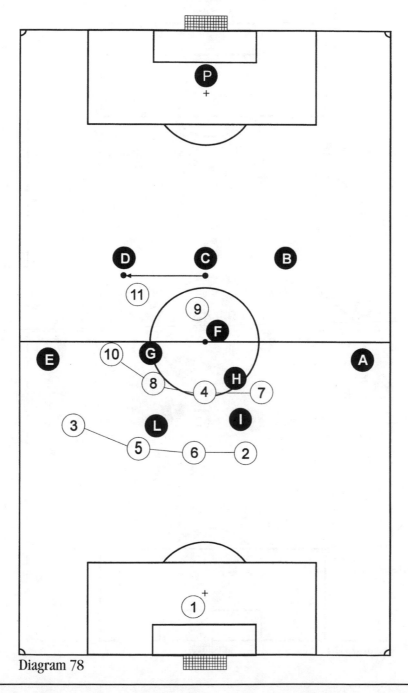

Diagram 78

ready to intercept an unlikely long pass to "A" in an attempt to switch the direction of the play, is also ready to rush forward if double-teaming (or pressure in general) leads to regaining possession of the ball. Double-teaming in the midfield right side zone (by the Right Side Midfielder and the Right Side Back) is not shown as its execution simply mirrors the one we have just described.

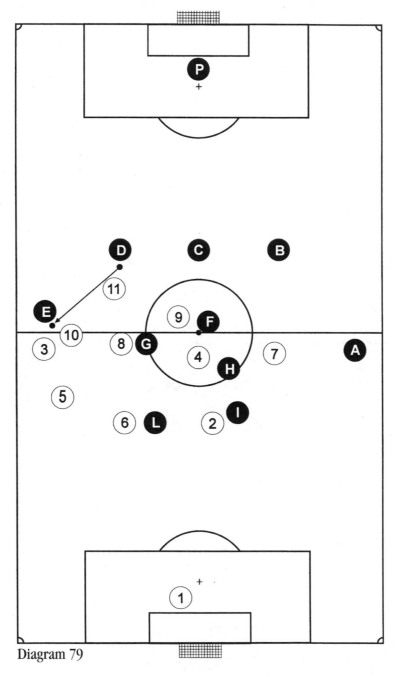

Diagram 79

## Double-Teaming in the Midfield Left Side Zone, Carried Out by the Left Side Midfielder and by a Forward

Diagram 78 shows a hypothetical opposing team, arranged according to a 5-3-2 pattern, for the purpose of training your team.

The exercise starts with the five opposing backs (A-B-C-D-E) who pass the ball between themselves from the right to the left and from the left to the right. While they do so, all the players of the team apply pressure; this means that when the ball is in possession of the three central players (B-C-D) forwards 9 and 11 will apply pressure, while when it is in "A's" possession number 7 will attack him; finally, when "E"'s in possession of the ball, number 10 will attack him.

When the ball goes from "C" to "D" (diagram 80) all the players will change their position according to the new position of the ball; in particular, if we want to apply double-teaming in the way we have explained before, number 9 follows the movement of the ball and is ready to rush to place himself between "D" and "E", while number 11 slowly goes towards the left.

Then, "D" passes the ball to "E" (diagram 81); double-teaming must be carried out during the time the ball takes to get from "D" to "E".

As diagram 81 shows, number 10 and 11 double-team while number 9 marks the back pass, number 8 marks the pass to the center and all the other players mark in advance the closest opponent; number 7, besides being ready to intercept an unlikely long pass to "A" to switch the direction of the play, is also ready to rush forward if double-teaming (or pressure in general) leads to regaining possession of the ball. Double-teaming in the midfield right side zone (by the Right Side Midfielder and a forward) is not shown as its execution simply mirrors the one we have just described.

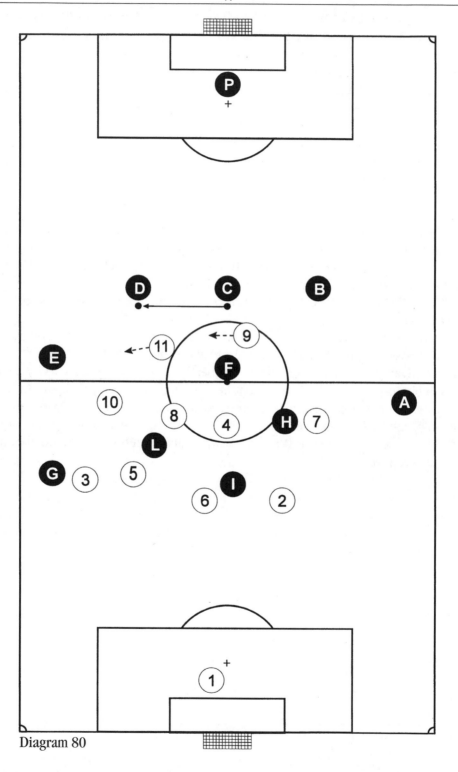

Diagram 80

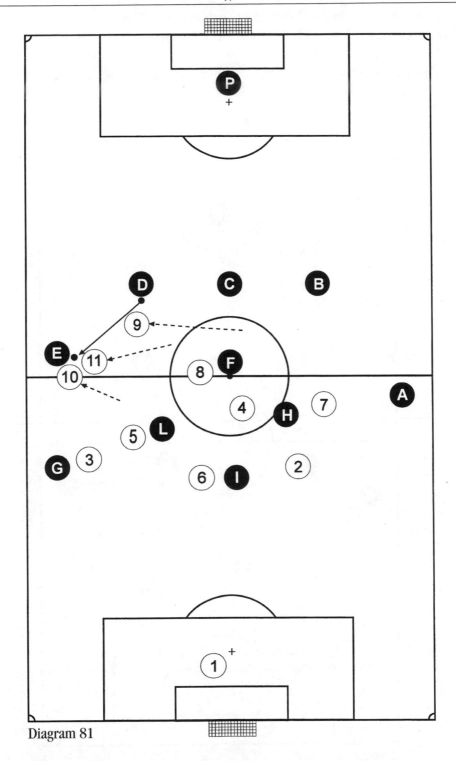

Diagram 81

## Double-Teaming in the Midfield Center-Right Zone, Carried Out By The Two Central Midfielders

Diagram 82 shows a hypothetical opposing team, arranged according to a 5-3-2 pattern, for the purpose of training your team.

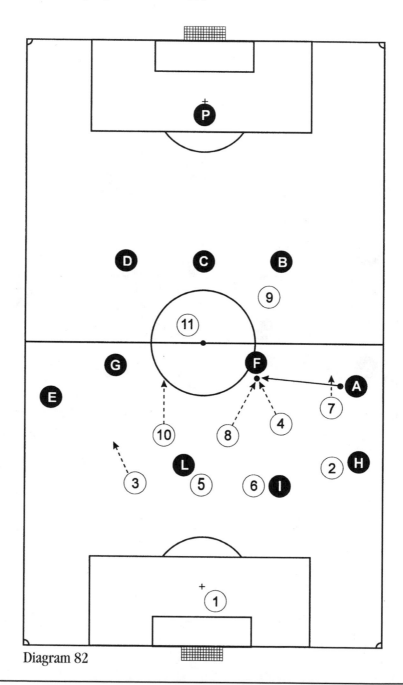

Diagram 82

The exercise starts with the opposing backs (A-B-C-D-E) who pass the ball between themselves continuously; when "A" gets the ball, he then passes it on to "F". When the ball is kicked by "A" towards "F" (diagram 82), the two central midfielders (number 4 and number 8) both attack the new player with the ball.

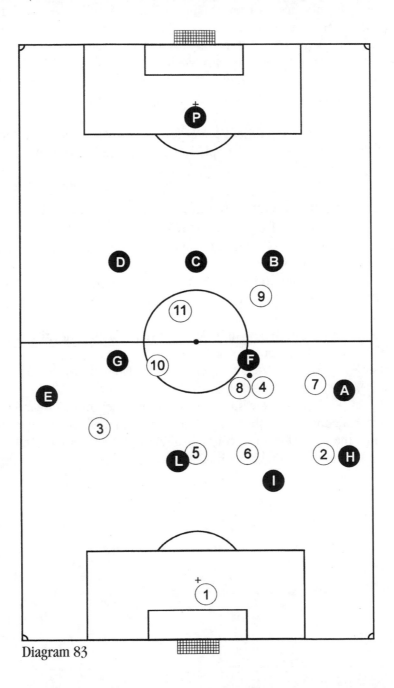

Diagram 83

*Double-teaming can be carried out if the ball from "A" to "F" is not very fast: in this case the midfielders gain time to stop the opponent: also, double-teaming can be applied in case of eventual difficulties in controlling the ball by "F".*

All the other players will try to shut all the possible passing lanes (see diagram 83); so number 7 marks "A" in advance and number 10 marks "G" in advance. The backs (number 2, 6 and 5) respectively mark in advance "H", "I" and "L", while number 3 moves forward and is ready to forestall or to stop "E" if the latter gets an unlikely pass from "F". The two forwards (number 9 and number 11) place themselves in a position enabling them to mark an eventual back pass to the backs.

Double-teaming in the midfield center-left zone (by the two central midfielders) is not shown as its execution simply mirrors the one we have just described.

## Double-Teaming in the Defensive Left Side Zone, Carried Out by the Left Side Back and the Left Side Midfielder

Diagram 84 shows a hypothetical opposing team, arranged according to a 5-3-2 pattern, for the purpose of training your team.

The exercise starts with the players of the opposing training team passing the ball freely between themselves, with light pressure by the team which will have to carry out the double-teaming.

When "G" gets the ball, he will have to (have previously decided to) pass the ball to "E" placed in an advanced side zone.

Number 3 and 10 double-team when the ball is passed by "G" towards "E" (diagram 84).

In diagram 85 we have the situation resulting when double-teaming is carried out; we can notice how "short" and "tight" the team is, and in particular how the backs and the midfielders are very close to each other, trying to have superiority in numbers in the zone where the ball is.

*Also, in diagram 85 we can see that number 8 is in an ideal position to attack the player with the ball; if this happens, we have triple-teaming on "G".*

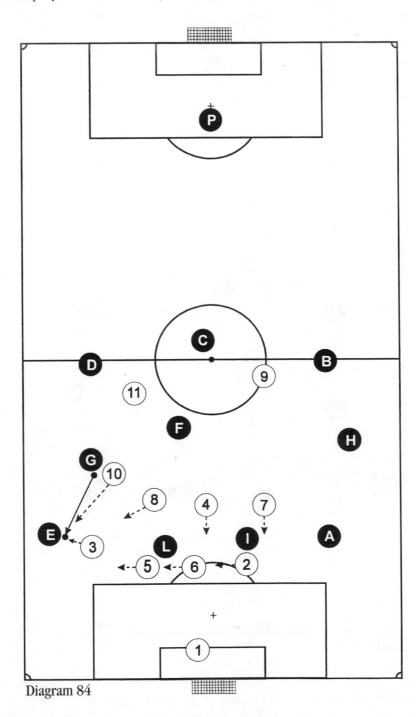

Diagram 84

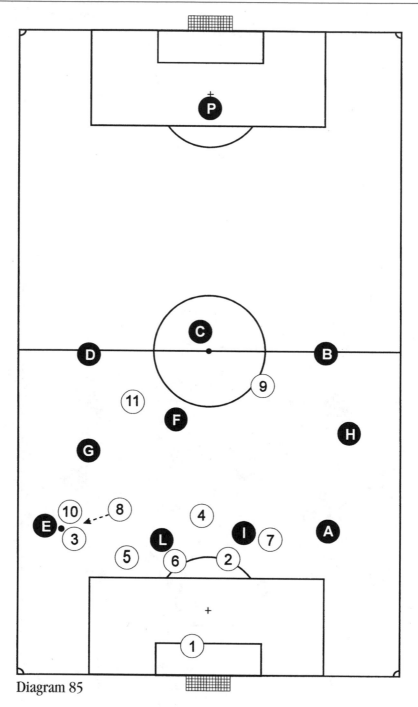

Diagram 85

Double-teaming in the defensive right side zone (by the Right Side Back and the Right Side Midfielder) is not shown as its execution simply mirrors the one we have just described.

# Double-Teaming in the Defensive Center-Left Zone, Carried Out by the Left Central Back and the Left Central Midfielder

Diagram 86 shows a hypothetical opposing team, arranged according to a 5-3-2 pattern, for the purpose of training your team.

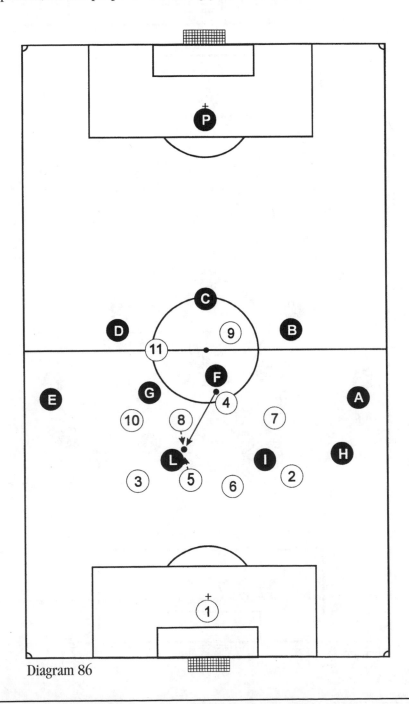

Diagram 86

The exercise starts with the players of the opposing training team passing the ball freely between themselves, with light pressure by the team which will have to carry out the double-teaming.

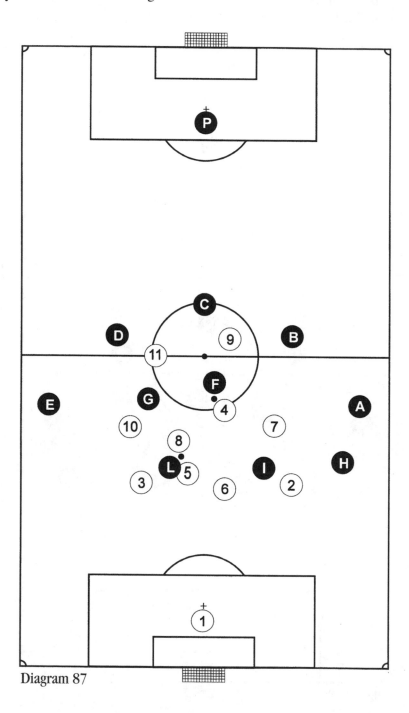

Diagram 87

When "F" gets the ball, he will have to (having previously decided to) pass the ball to forward "L" (diagram 86).

Number 5 and 8 double-team when the ball is kicked by "F" towards "L".

In diagram 87 we have the situation resulting when double-teaming is carried out; we can notice how "short" and "tight" the team is, and in particular how the backs and the midfielders are very close to each other, trying to have superiority in numbers in the zone where the ball is.

Double-teaming in the defensive center-right zone (by the Right Central Back and the Right Central Midfielder) is not shown as its execution simply mirrors the one we have just described.

# 6

# Application of Off-Side Tactics

In diagram 88, A-B-B1-B2-C1-C2 we have indicated sectors of your half of the field, with the aim of pointing out the area within which the application of the off-side tactics, after a clearance and with the simultaneous application of pressure, has good chances of success or, better, generates acceptable risks.

In our opinion, area A (central zone), is the least risky area to apply the off-side trap after a clearance from the backs, because it is the one with the highest concentration of your players.

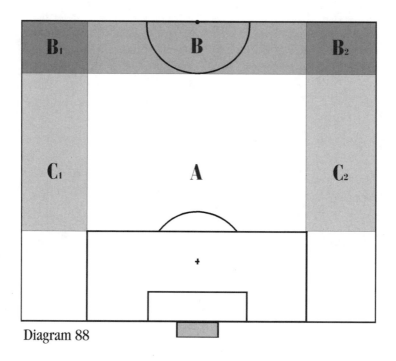

Diagram 88

Let's imagine a clearance from one of your backs with the ball directed anywhere within area A; we can count on at least three or four players to apply pressure on that ball and they, thanks to the coordinated forward movement of the backs, will regain possession of the ball either thanks to an indirect free-kick leaving one or more opponents off-side or taking the ball away from the opponents through the application of pressure.

As area B is a central zone it could seem suitable to the application of the off-side trap, but it is not because it is not a zone with a high concentration of your players; in fact, if the ball is cleared from your penalty area at most we can have one or both forwards in area B; therefore, the application of pressure becomes difficult if we consider that the midfielders who could apply pressure in that area would inevitably be late.

We should also keep in mind that off-side is whistled for from the midfield line on, so its application near the midfield line generates too high a risk if compared to our aim which is to regain possession of the ball. It is important, but it must not be pursued through situations which could determine a negative outcome of the game.

Side zones C1 and C2 are not suitable for the application of the off-side trap because only one or two players, after the ball has been cleared towards these zones, can attack the opponent with the ball while the others move forward. In other words, the number of the players applying pressure is unlikely to guarantee the regaining of the ball, and the high risk that the player with the ball may dribble past the one(s) trying to stop him, thus running undisturbed towards the goal, does not recommend the application of pressure here. The application of off-side is similarly not to be recommended if the ball is cleared towards zones B1 and B2 because in such areas there are the same problems as in zone B and in zones C1 and C2.

## Application of the Off-Side Tactics When the Ball is Cleared Towards Zone A

In diagram 89 we have such an example: after the pass from opponent "A", number 6 clears and opponent "F" gets the ball; he is attacked by the closer players (in this case there are five, numbers 4-8-2-6-5) while those farther away move forward in order to leave their opponents off-side.

The resulting situation is shown in diagram 89.1.

The application of the off-side tactics after a corner kick with a clearance towards a central zone (zone A) is shown as it is similar to the situations of picture 89 and 89.1.

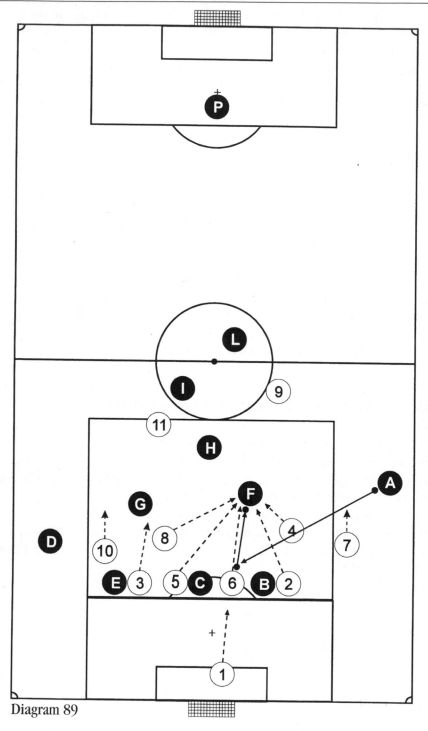

Diagram 89

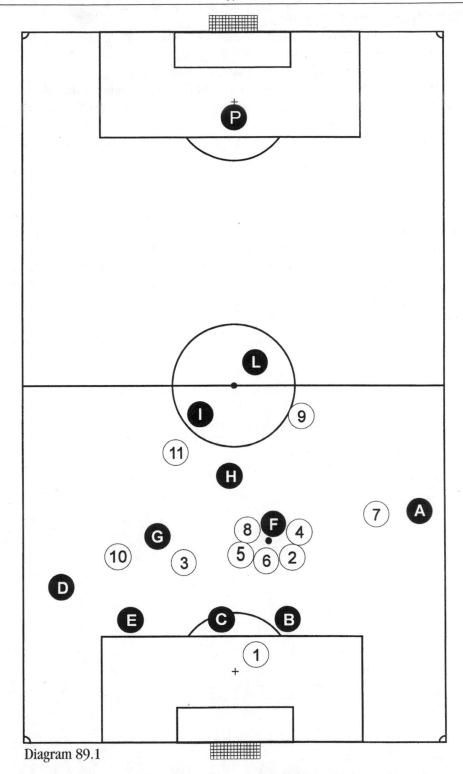

Diagram 89.1

## Ball Cleared Towards Zone C1

Diagram 90 shows what can happen when the ball is cleared towards side zone C1 (the same considerations apply for zone C2: opponent "A" cross-passes the ball, cleared by back 3 towards zone C1, where opponent "D" gets it.

**If what figure 90 shows came true, that is if number 10 and 3 attacked "D" and the other defending players moved forward in order to leave the opponents off-side, there would be a 1 against 2 situation ("D" against number 10 and 3) in which "D" could be successful, running with the ball towards the goal undisturbed.**

*In this particular situation it is better to do what diagram 90.1 shows: number 10 and 3 apply pressure on "D", while the other backs (as well as the midfielders) do not move forward in order to apply off-side: they move towards the opponent with the ball, in order to close up the team.*

If the clearance of number 3 towards zone C1 had been longer and deeper the players would have placed themselves in the same way with the only difference that, in order to keep the team short and tight, the backs and the midfielders, besides moving towards the ball, should have moved some yards forward, but without applying the off-side tactics.

In diagram 90.1, forwards "E", "C" and "B" have remained behind the backs; so, if "D", avoiding the pressure applied by number 10 and 3, manages to pass the ball in depth to one of the three forwards, they will be off-side due to the simple group movement aimed at closing up the team.

They are unlikely to regain possession of the ball as a result of an indirect free kick, as with the only movement aimed at closing up the team the forwards may have the time to regain their regular position.

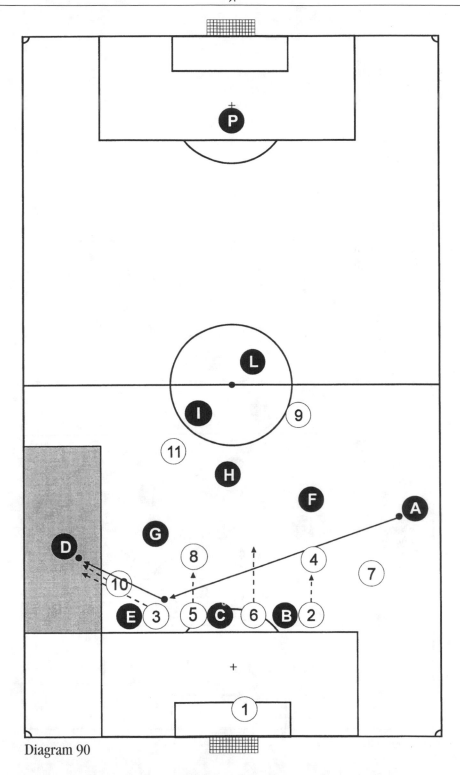

Diagram 90

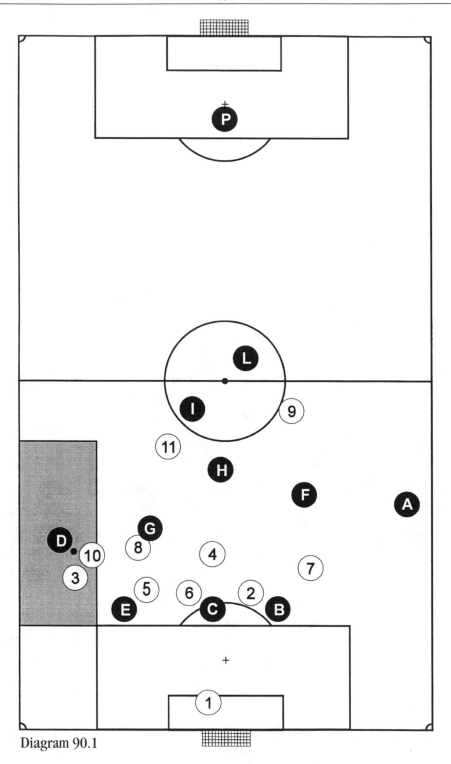

Diagram 90.1

## Ball Cleared Towards Zone B

In diagram 91 the ball is cleared towards zone B. Opponent A cross-passes to the center, towards the attacking third of the field or towards the limit of your penalty area; the left central back, number 5, clears the ball towards the zone of opponent "F" (central zone near the midfield line - zone B).

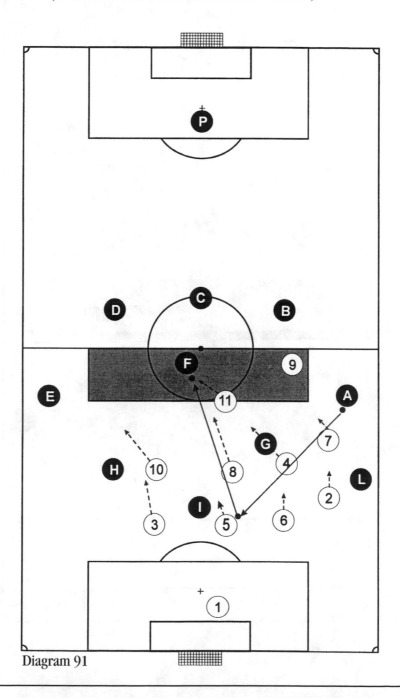

Diagram 91

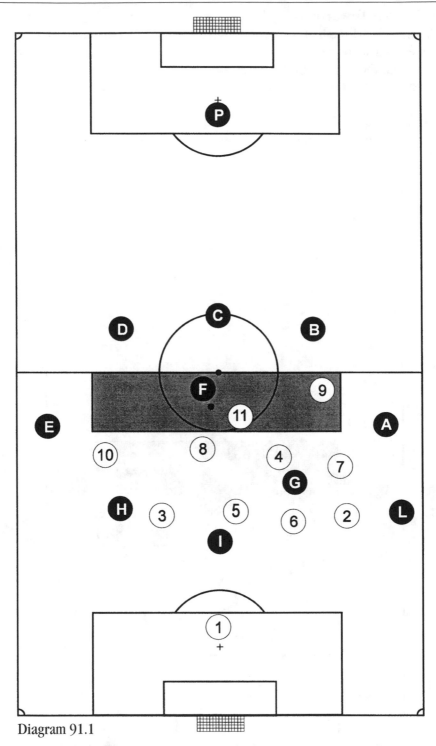

Diagram 91.1

When "F" gets possession of the ball only number 11 is in a position to attack him because he is nearby, while forward 9 and midfielders 10 and 8 are not close enough to the player with the ball to be able to carry out suitable pressure.

Diagram 91.1 shows the suitable arrangement in the situation considered: number 11 attacks "F", number 8 double-teams "F", number 10 places himself in a position enabling him to mark "E" in advance and all the other players shorten their distance from the ball according to the position of the player with the ball, without applying the off-side tactics.

In diagram 91.1 forward "I" has remained behind all the backs, so if "F" passes the ball towards him he will be off-side due to the simple group movement aimed at closing up the team, without applying the off-side trap.

"I" is unlikely to remain behind the backs because with the only movement aimed at closing up the team the forward may have the time to regain his regular position.

## Application of the Off-Side Tactics Directly on a Free Kick

Diagram 92 shows the application of the off-side tactics on a free kick, when the ball is passed towards your penalty area.

If we sense that the opponent about to take the free kick will make a long pass forward, the backs and the other defending players will place themselves along the same line as the opponent that they are marking. After having previously agreed on it, they will move forward at the moment when the opposing player who is going to take the free kick starts to kick the ball.

In diagram 92 we can see how, at the moment when opponent "B" starts to kick the ball, backs 2-6-5-3 and the defending players move forward in order to leave the opponents off-side.

The situation resulting from the application of the off-side trap is shown in diagram 92.1.

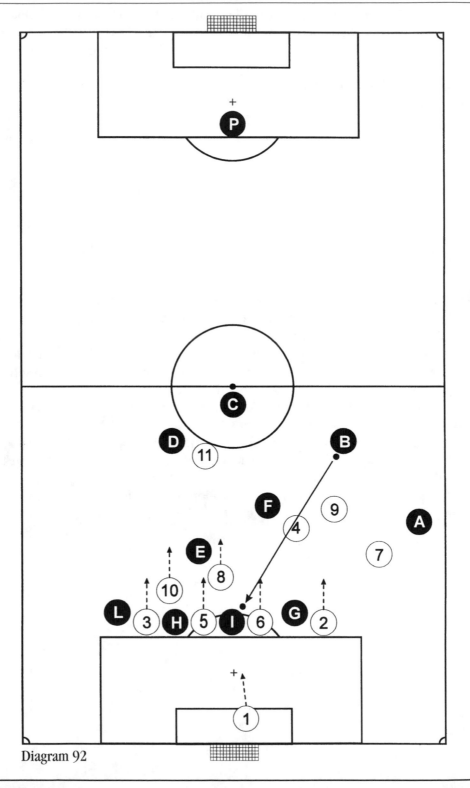

Diagram 92

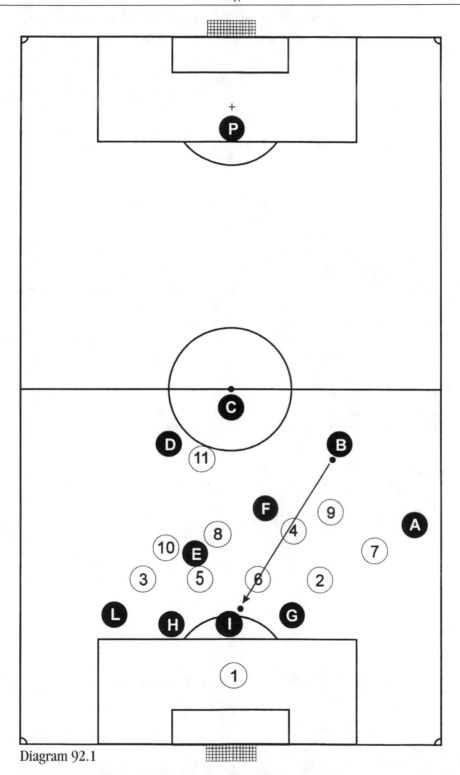

Diagram 92.1

## Application of the Off-Side Tactics When the Forward, with the Goal at his Back, Makes A Back Pass

In diagram 93 forward "L" gets the ball with the goal at his back and, attacked by two opponents (see diagram 93.1), makes a back pass to his teammate "F". At the very moment when "L" makes the back pass to "F" (diagram 93.2), the midfielders closer to "F" (8 and 4) apply pressure on him and also the backs closer to "F" (numbers 3, 5 and 6) attack the player with the ball; the other midfielders (number 7 and 10) and the other back (number 2), more distant from the player with the ball, move forward in order to leave the opposing forwards off-side.

In diagram 93.2 we can see the movement that the players have to make at the moment when the back pass takes place, while diagram 93.3 shows the resulting situation.

*According to the resulting situation that we have shown, if pressure is successful your team regains possession of the ball; if "F" manages to pass the ball deep your team regains possession of the ball as well with an indirect free kick; finally, if player "F" manages to pass the ball to "A" (this is probably his only chance not to lose the ball) some players (those closer to "A", that is numbers 4, 6 and 5) among those applying pressure on "F" must re-arrange themselves on the new player with the ball and attack him, helped by the other players who have moved forward (number 7 and number 2) and who find themselves close to opponent "A" in the new situation.*

The sequence of diagrams 93-93.1-93.2-93.3 shows the evolution of the application of the off-side tactics in this specific situation.

*Arrigo Sacchi makes a point to the Italian team during training for the 1996 European Championships.*

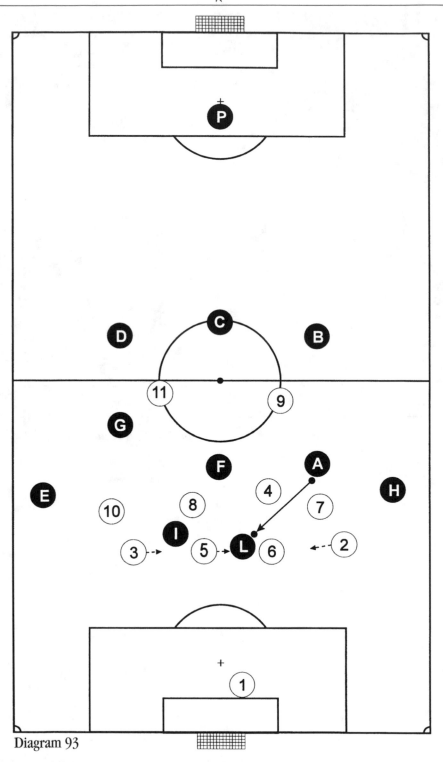

Diagram 93

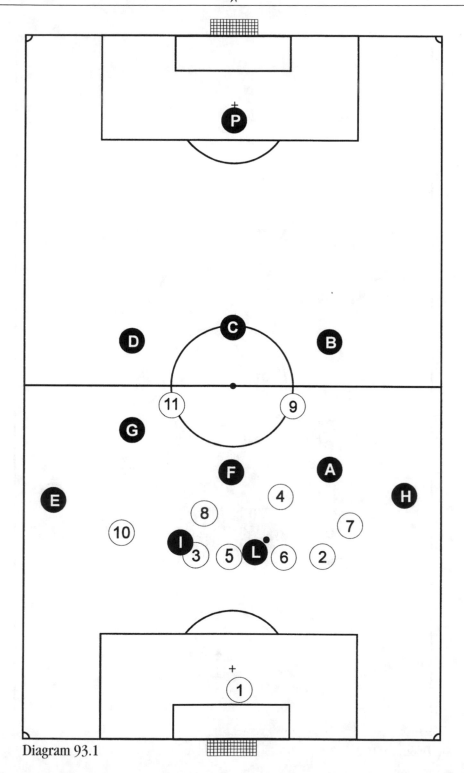

Diagram 93.1

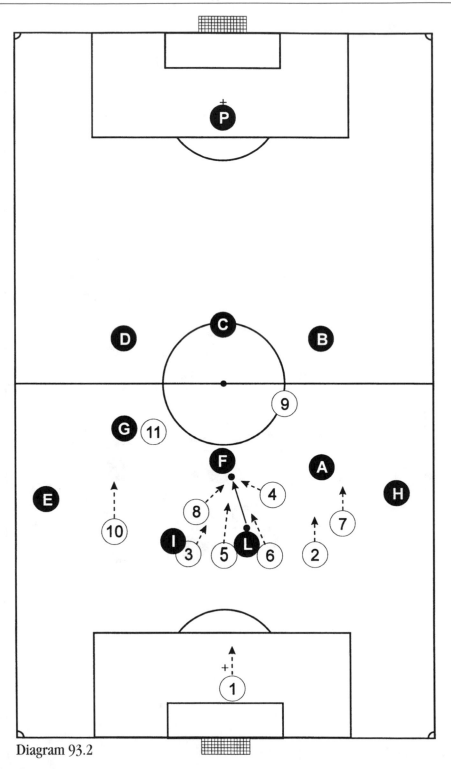

Diagram 93.2

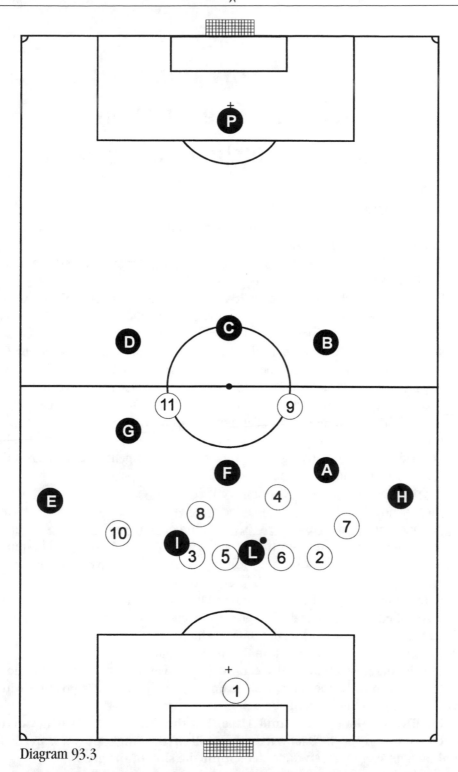

Diagram 93.3

# 7

# Defensive Organization
# Aimed At Starting An Attack

## Organized Attack

As we have already said, zone play is primarily defensive tactics aiming at regaining possession of the ball.

Of course, once the ball has been regained a well-organized and previously prepared attack will have to be carried out.

In zone play, each player belongs to a certain area; so, when a player regains possession of the ball, he and all his teammates are in their own usual area (with possible shifts due to the position of the opponent with the ball). This fact is an advantage to start an attack: as all the players are in their natural positions (the ones they are more suitable for) they can give their best and carry out immediate attacks, prepared and tried out during the training sessions as detailed in Chapter 9. So, once the team has regained possession of the ball in a certain area, it will be ready to start an immediate attack according to a scheme arranged beforehand. In case this is not possible because of the opponents' arrangement, the ball can be made to circulate trying to find useful zones to penetrate, using another scheme prepared in practice.

If your opponents are well-organized, it is not easy to develop attacking schemes identical to the ones studied and tried out during the training sessions. The primary aim of the attacking scheme is to generate in the players a "group mentality" which puts the team (the group) above the single player. The repetition of certain schemes during the training sessions also gives the players an imprint of the kind of play the coach intends to carry out.

In this context, the skill of the single player has perhaps a higher value than in the so-called traditional play. The good or even the first-rate player placing his skill at the group's disposal can determine a higher performance of his team even with solutions of play different from the prepared ones.

Developing a group mentality can mean, for example, to carry out a movement in order to make room for one's teammate, switching one's position with a teammate on purpose or out of necessity, etc.

**Finally, we would like to underline that the skill of a team is not determined by the group in itself: it is the skill of the single players, perfectly combined among themselves, to determine the skill of the group.**

In zone play the player must be prepared to perform "total" soccer, in which he must take part both in the defensive and in the attacking phase; as a consequence, he must have the necessary technical, athletic and physical characteristics, but above all he must have very good tactical skills.

## Exercise to Make the Ball Circulate Between the Back Four

Because of obvious safety reasons, the ball should never circulate parallel to the midfield line: it should be passed from one back to the other in such a way as to make the trajectory of the ball form an angle to the horizontal axis of the field. In order to make this happen, the back four must place themselves according to a "half-moon" formation.

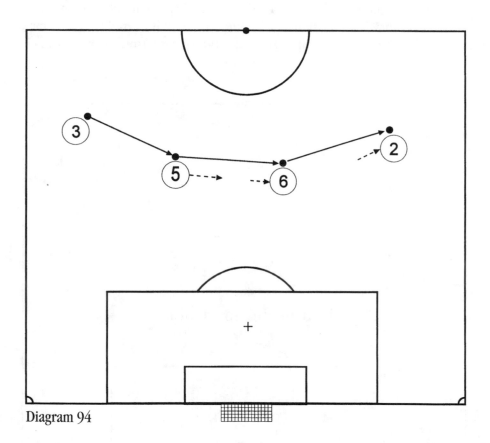

Diagram 94

When the backs regain possession of the ball, they are within the strong side; therefore, besides making the ball circulate towards the opposite side (as it is presumably free from opponents), they must move towards that side in such a way as to place themselves uniformly on the field.

In diagram 94 we can see that, after number 3 has regained possession of the ball, number 5, number 6 and number 2 move towards the right-hand side of the field in order to get the ball.

To get the backs used to making the ball circulate we recommend an exercise with the back four placed as shown in diagram 95, where the ball is made to circulate from the left to the right, or as shown in diagram 95.1, where the ball is made to circulate from the right to the left.

The difference between these two arrangements is that, while in the circulation of the ball from the left to the right (diagram 95) it is number 6 who slightly parts from the "half-moon", in the circulation of the ball from the right to the left (diagram 95.1) it is number 5, instead, who slightly parts from such a formation.

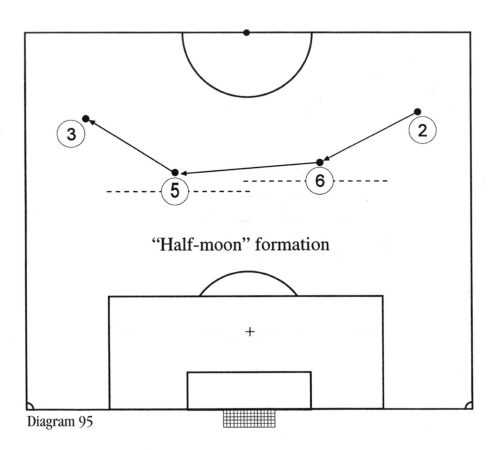

"Half-moon" formation

Diagram 95

When the ball is made to go from one side of the field to the other, each back should pass the ball to the nearest back in order to avoid the interception of long passes by the opponents; also, the backs must play the ball with only two touches. For example, if the ball is circulating from the left to the right the two central backs must control it with the inside of their right foot and pass it with the inside of their left foot, while the two side backs must control the ball and pass it with the same foot, in both directions of circulation; therefore, number 3 will use his left foot for both operations, while number 2 will use his right foot.

When the ball circulates from the right to the left, the two central backs must control it with the inside of their left foot and pass it with the inside of their right foot.

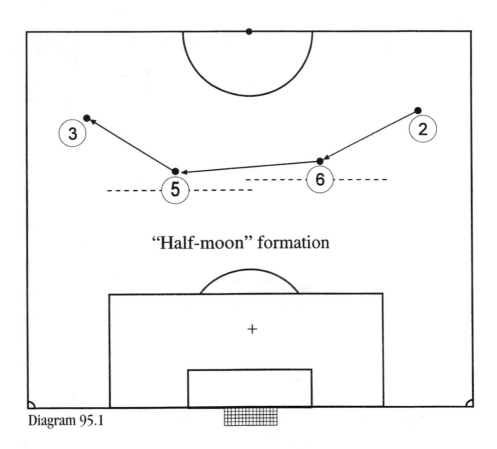

"Half-moon" formation

Diagram 95.1

## Exercise to Make the Ball Circulate Between the Back Four, with the Support of a central Midfielder

The back four must arrange themselves as shown either in diagram 95 or in diagram 95.1, according to the direction of circulation of the ball.

In addition, a central midfielder places himself in front of the line of the backs, moving from the left to the right and vice versa in the same direction as the ball.

The exercise starts (diagram 96) with the backs passing the ball to each other; when the coach whistles (pre-established signal), the back with the ball (number 2 in diagram 96) passes the ball to the central midfielder (number 4) who, with one or two touches, passes the ball to the next back (number 6 in this example) making it circulate.

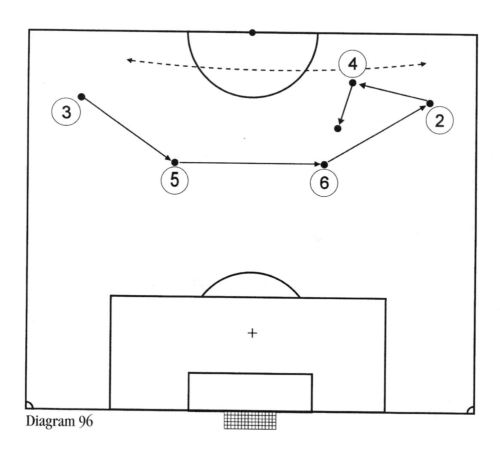

Diagram 96

The exercise continues as shown in diagram 96.1; after getting the ball, number 6 passes it to number 5 who, after hearing the coach's whistle while the ball was reaching him, passes it to the central midfielder (number 4) who passes it to number 3. Number 3 will then start the circulation of the ball in the reverse direction, that is from the left to the right.

The same exercise must be done again, with the same characteristics, placing the other central midfielder (number 8) in front of the defending line.

Later, the same exercise can be done without the signal of the coach: the players themselves will decide when to pass the ball to the central midfielder. The exercise can be further expanded by inserting one or more opponents.

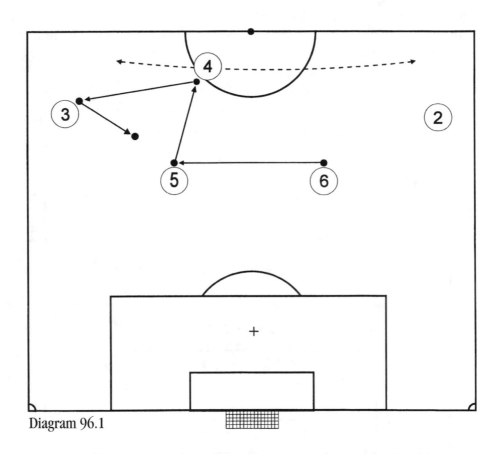

Diagram 96.1

## Exercise to Make the Ball Circulate Between the Back Four, with the Support of Both Central Midfielders

This exercise is to be carried out with the same logic used for the circulation of the ball between the back four supported by a central midfielder.

The exercise starts with the players arranged as shown in diagram 97. The circulation of the ball between the backs starts from the left to the right; when the coach whistles, number 6 passes the ball to the right central midfielder (number 4) who passes it to number 2.

The exercise continues as shown in diagram 97.1. After getting the ball, number 2 passes it to number 6 who, after hearing the coach's whistle, passes the ball back to the right central midfielder (number 4) who passes it to number 5. Number 5, after the coach's whistle, passes the ball to the left central midfielder (number 8). In turn, number 8 passes the ball to number 3, who starts to make the ball circulate back.

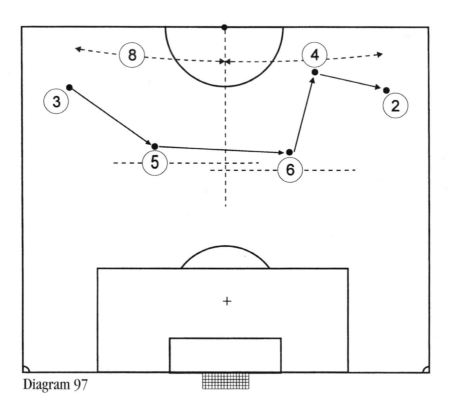

Diagram 97

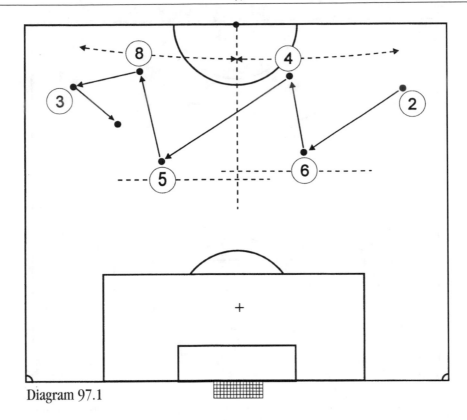

Diagram 97.1

Of course the sequence of the passes between backs and midfielders depends on the signals by the coach; therefore, this kind of practice serves only to consolidate and reinforce the skills and tactics involved to retain possession and create attacking opportunities.

It is important to notice that the two central midfielders are respectively in the zones where they belong.

Later, this exercise can also be done without the signal of the coach. Of course, in presence of the opponents the players will carry out suitable passes according to the situations of play.

### Exercise to Make the Ball Circulate Along the Defending Line, Leaving Out One of the Central Backs

In this exercise the back four place themselves according to a half-moon formation. As diagram 98 shows, the ball circulates from the left to the right, starting with number 3 who passes the ball to number 5, who does not pass the ball to the other central back (number 6) but passes it directly to number 2.

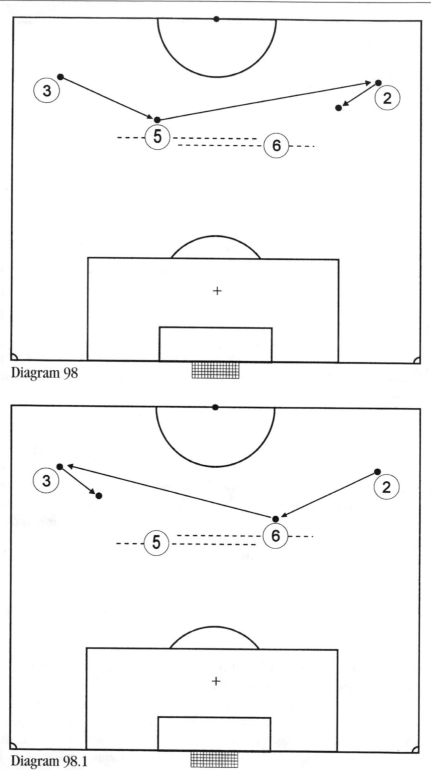

Diagram 98

Diagram 98.1

The exercise continues as shown in diagram 98.1, with the ball circulating in the reverse manner; number 2 passes it to number 6, who does not pass the ball to the other central back (number 5) but passes it directly to number 3.

Such a move could be dangerous during a game because a long side pass could enable the opponents to intercept the ball, so it will be applied only when there is necessity to speed up the game, when the opponents have almost no chance to intercept the ball and when there is a useful corridor on one of the sides.

## Exercise to Make the Ball Circulate Along the Defending Line, with Interchange Between the Right Central Back and the Right Side Back, or Between the Left Central Back and the Left Side Back

This exercise is shown in diagram 99, with the back four arranged according to a half-moon formation.

The ball starts circulating from the left to the right, number 3  passes it to number 5. While the ball is on its way to number 5, the right side back (number 2) and the right central back (number 6) interchange their positions; after getting the ball, number 5 passes it to the right central back who has moved to a side position (see diagram 99.1).

The exercise continues in diagram 99.2, with player number 6 who passes the ball to number 2 (who has remained in a central position) who, in turn, passes the ball to the left central back who has interchanged his position with the left side back (see diagram 99.3).

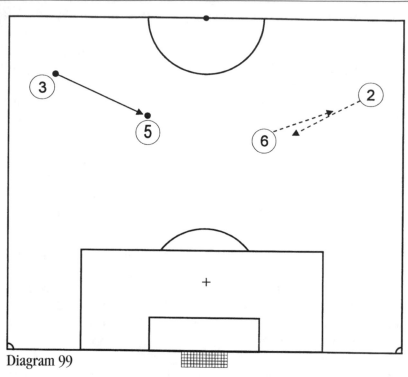

Diagram 99

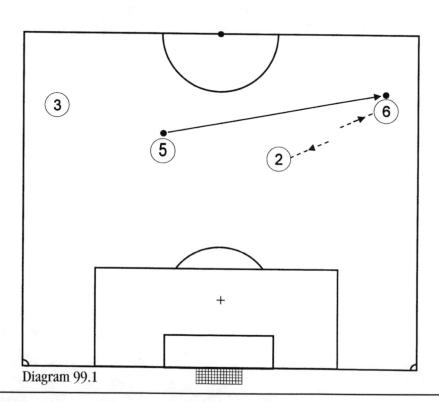

Diagram 99.1

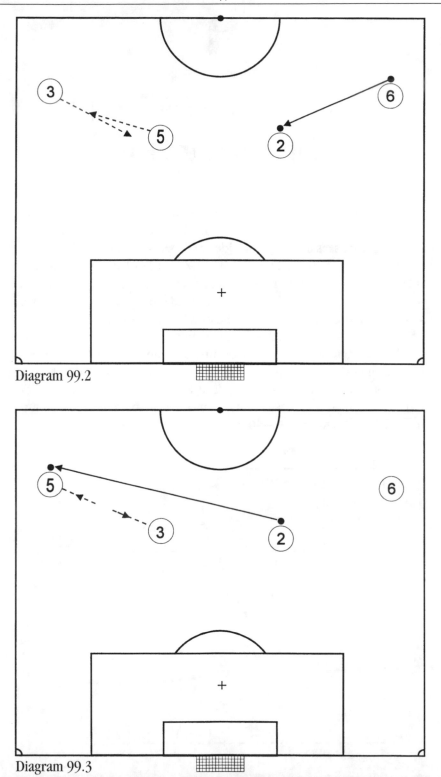

Diagram 99.2

Diagram 99.3

# 8

# Conventional Movements
# of the Forward Pair

**Criss-Crossing**

In diagram 100 the two forwards criss-cross in the attacking third of the field. This allows two possible passes, pointed out by the two eventual trajectories of the ball in possession of midfielder number 8, as shown by lines a and b. The ideal moment to pass the ball is when the profile of the more advanced forward hides behind the profile of the other forward.

In diagram 100.1 the two forwards, just inside the penalty area, criss-cross at the moment when the cross-pass from the end line is about to be made.

In the criss-crossing movement it is always the forward who can see both the ball and his teammate who has to adapt himself, subordinating his movement to the choice of the other forward. If, as in the example of diagram 100.1, number 11 decided not to criss-cross but, instead, to head for the nearer post, then number 9, who can see both the ball and the movement of number 11, must adapt himself and consequently head for the far post.

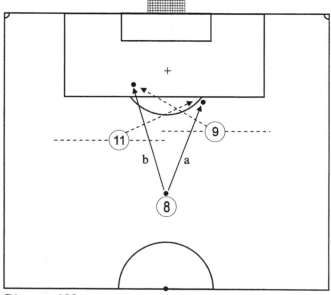

Diagram 100

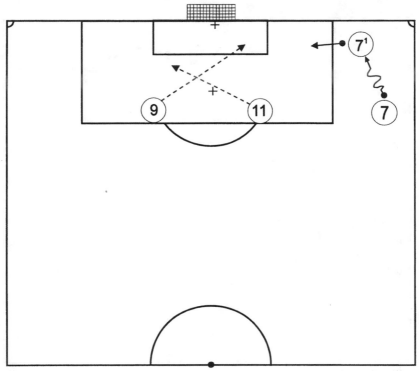

Diagram 100.1

## Diversion

With this term we mean the contemporaneous movement of the two forwards towards the side lines; the forward closer to the right side line (number 9 in the example of picture 101) goes towards the right while the one closer to the left side line (number 11) goes towards the left.

This movement is particularly helpful when the opponents mark your forwards man-to-man because you can make room in the middle for the throwing forward of your midfielders.

In the diversion it is always the forward who can see both the ball and his teammate who has to adapt himself as to the movement to make. In the example of diagram 101, number 11 decides to move to the left side of the attacking front. As a consequence, number 9 moves to the reverse side and thus they make room in the middle for the simultaneous throwing forward of midfielder 4, who will receive a deep pass from the player with the ball, number 8. In this kind of move it is fundamental to choose the right time to carry out the various movements.

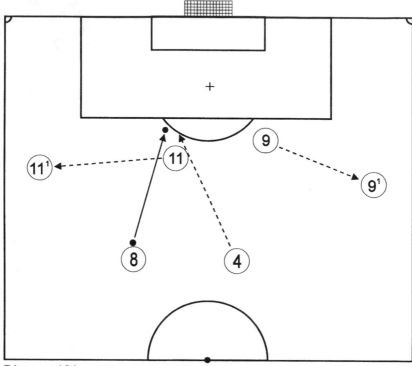

Diagram 101

## Diagonal

In the diagonal movement the two forwards move to the same side line at the same time. The aim, like in the diversion, is to free the central zone of attack, provided the opponents mark your two forwards man-to-man.

In the example of diagram 102, player number 8, thanks to the diagonal movement, can pass the ball to number 4, throwing him into the presumably free area. In the diagonal movement it is always the forward who can see both the ball and his teammate who has to comply with the pre-established movement. In the example of diagram 102, number 9 can see both the ball and his teammate; so, when number 11 decides to move to the side, number 9 will have to move in the same direction.

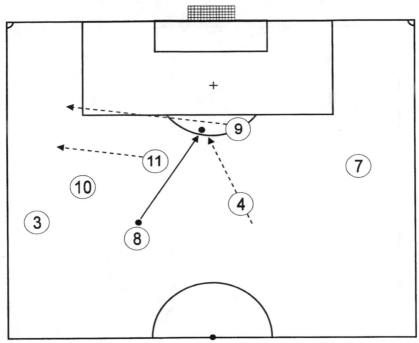

Diagram 102

## "L" Shaped Movement

It is called "L" shaped movement because the two forwards "draw" this letter of the alphabet with their movement. As we can see from the two different examples (diagrams 103 and 103.1), it has the aim of making room for either one of the two forwards (in diagram 103, number 11, who receives a pass from number 4 in the area left free by number 9) or for a midfielder (in diagram 103.1 number 10 throws himself forward into the area left by number 11 who has gone to occupy the area left free by number 9 who, in turn, has gone towards the ball).

In the example shown in diagram 103.1, number 4 passes the ball to number 9 who passes it backward to number 8; then number 8 passes the ball deep to midfielder number 10 in the presumably free area.

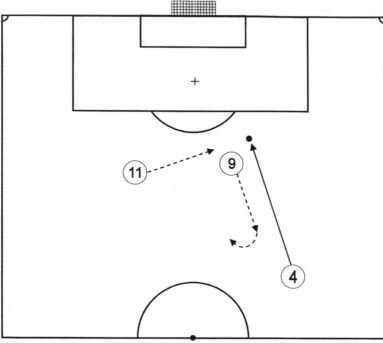

Diagram 103

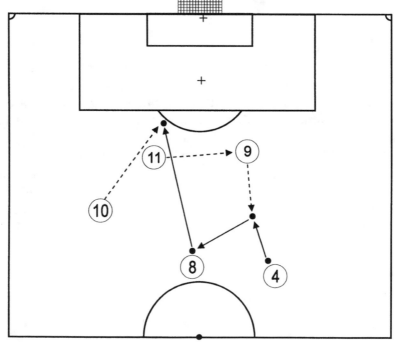

Diagram 103.1

## Reverse Move

Diagram 104 shows a movement of the forwards called the "reverse move". The forward who can see both the ball and his teammate must comply with the movement made by the teammate himself.

In diagram 104, number 11 can see the ball and number 9; therefore, if number 9 cuts towards the right (this trajectory is indicated by letter a) number 11 will cut towards the left (this trajectory is indicated by letter a); instead, if number 9 goes towards the ball (trajectory b) number 11 will go deep, following trajectory b; finally, if number 9 follows trajectory c, number 11 will follow "his" trajectory c, going towards the ball.

The two forwards move according to a reverse move, following parallel trajectories.

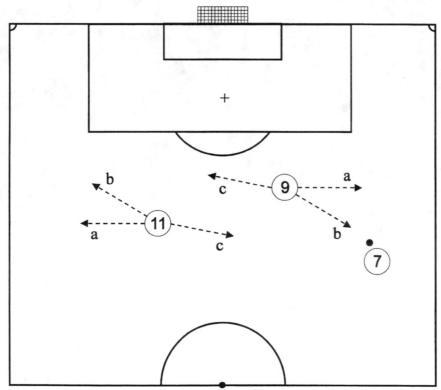

Diagram 104

*Albertini and Castacurta double team rushes Kolyvanov in Euro '96.*

# 9

# Attack Schemes

## Attack Schemes 11 v 0

In the following pages you can find 19 attacking "schemes" which we would prefer to define as organized movements to prepare an attack, aiming at shooting at goal.

We would not like to define our attacking proposals as schemes, because if interpreted in an extremely strict way they could be restrictive to imagination in particular in the final phase of their application where the presence of the opponent strongly affects the move.

Bearing in mind that such proposals are studied and practiced during the training sessions without opponents (11 versus 0), we think that it is easier to apply a pre-established plan in the initial part of the attack, provided the opponents allow it during the game. In the final part of the attack we think that room should be made for the inventiveness and the creativity of the individual player, depending on the occurring situation (it is not by chance that soccer has been defined the situational sport par excellence). As a consequence, most of our attacking proposals - which we will inaccurately call schemes - do not give a complete solution for the final part of the attack.

We have not described the schemes; however, examples are given in two different phases and with easy to read diagrams.

In the first diagram of each scheme we have given examples from the beginning of the attack, aimed at carrying out a pre-established plan. In the second diagram we have the subsequent development of the same scheme, with the exception, as we have already said, of the shooting at goal. Each single attacking scheme can be understood immediately, as the two diagrams are next to each other.

All 19 schemes have been conceived, and examples given, with movements on the right or center-right zone of the field. Of course. each scheme can be executed in a mirror way on the left or center-left zone of the field.

## Scheme 1 first part

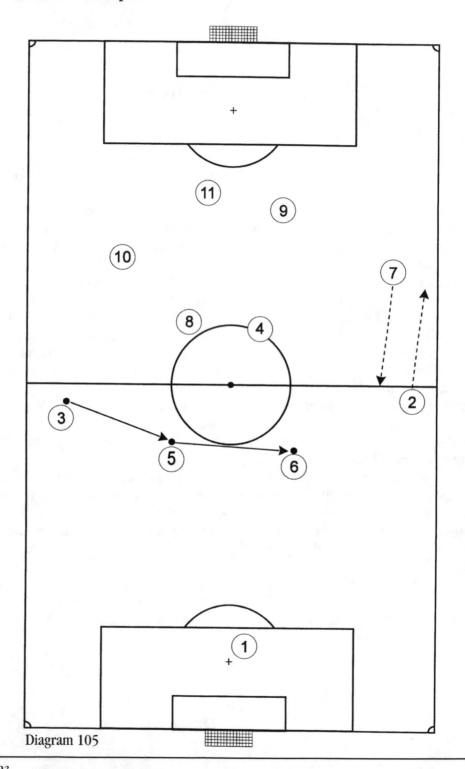

Diagram 105

## Scheme 1 second part

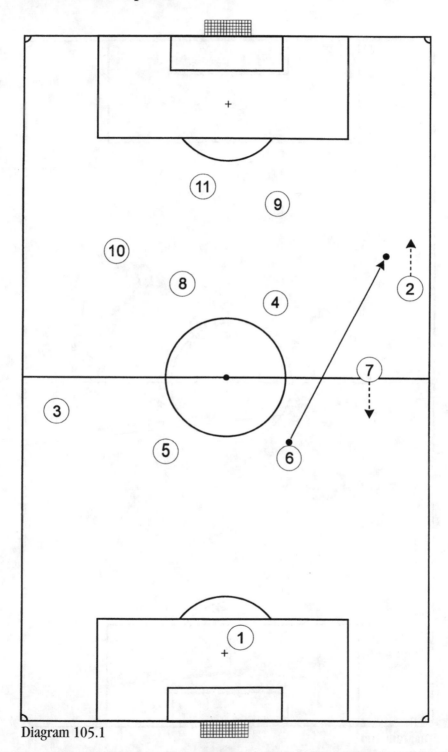

Diagram 105.1

# Scheme 2 first part

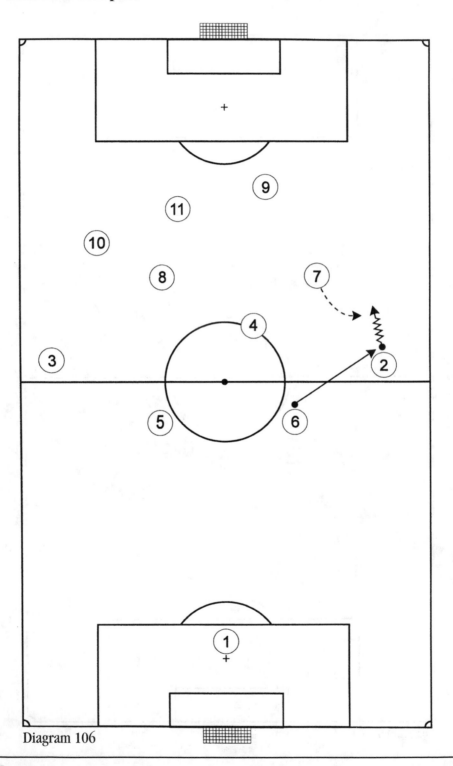

Diagram 106

# Scheme 2 second part

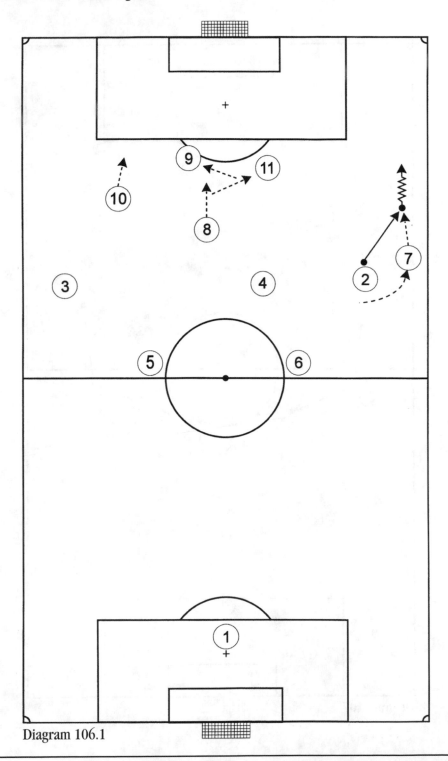

Diagram 106.1

# Scheme 3 first part

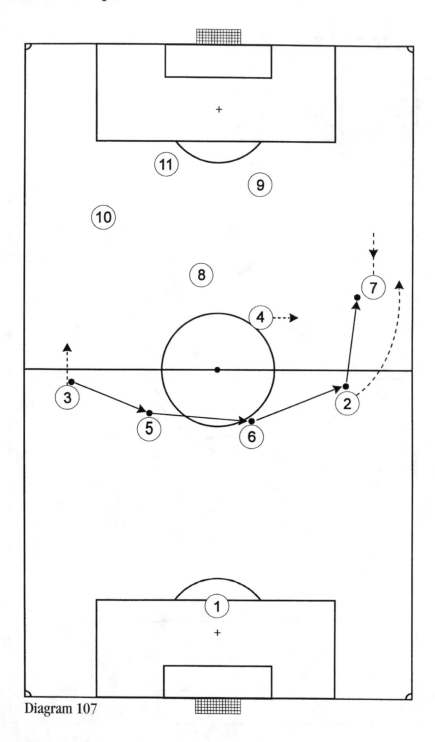

Diagram 107

**Scheme 3 second part**

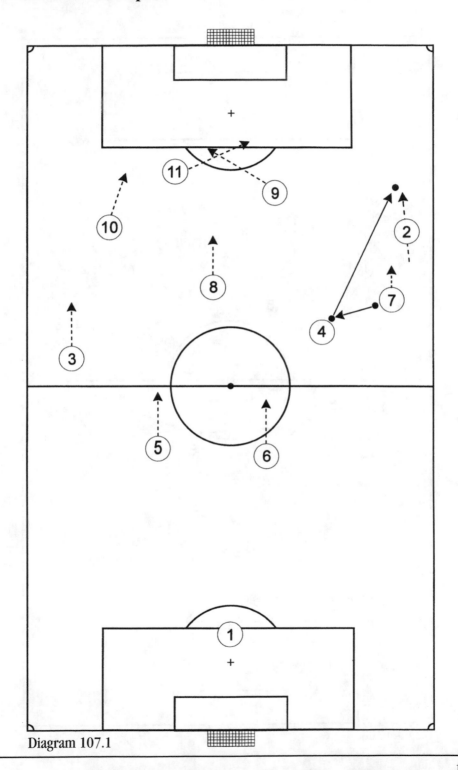

Diagram 107.1

**Scheme 4 first part**

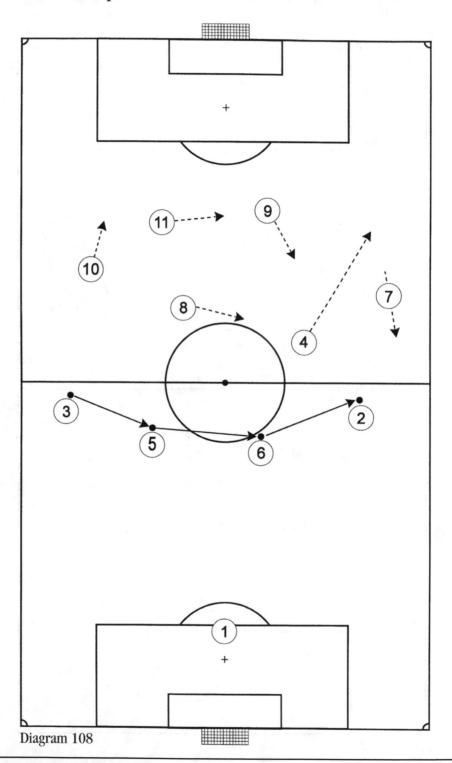

Diagram 108

Scheme 4 second part

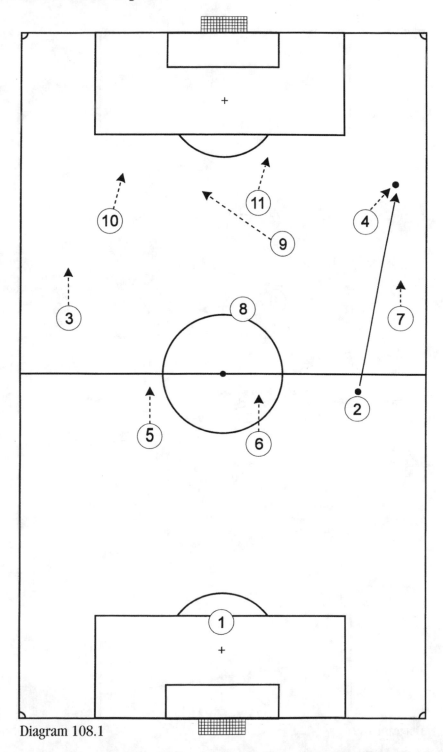

Diagram 108.1

# Scheme 5 first part

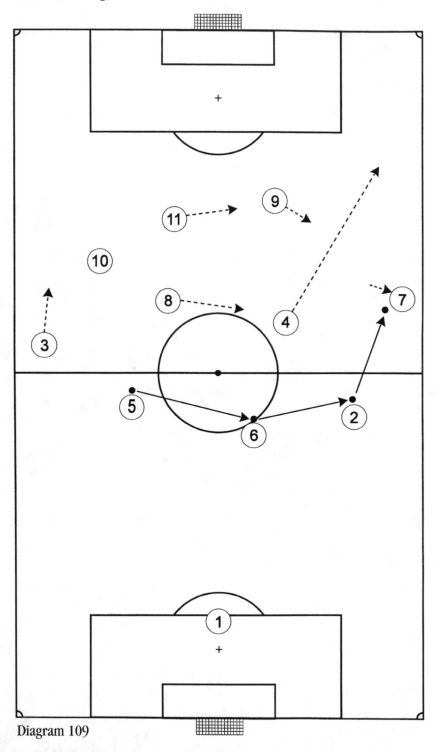

Diagram 109

# Scheme 5 second part

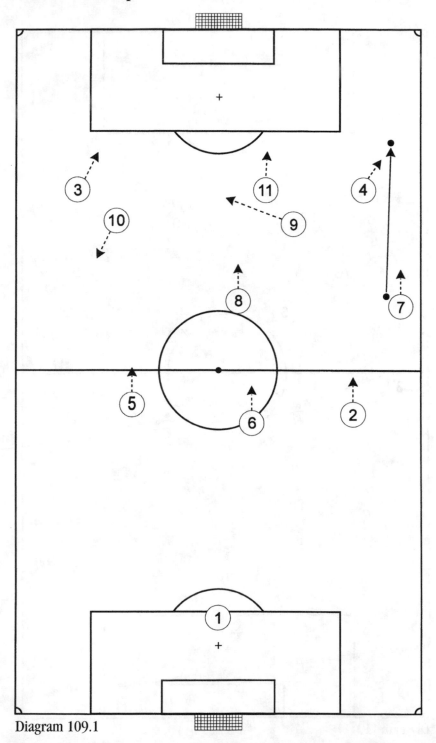

Diagram 109.1

# Scheme 6 first part

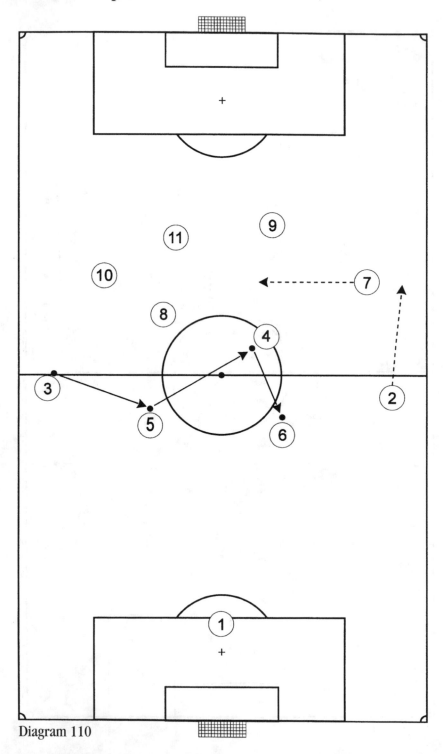

Diagram 110

# Scheme 6 second part

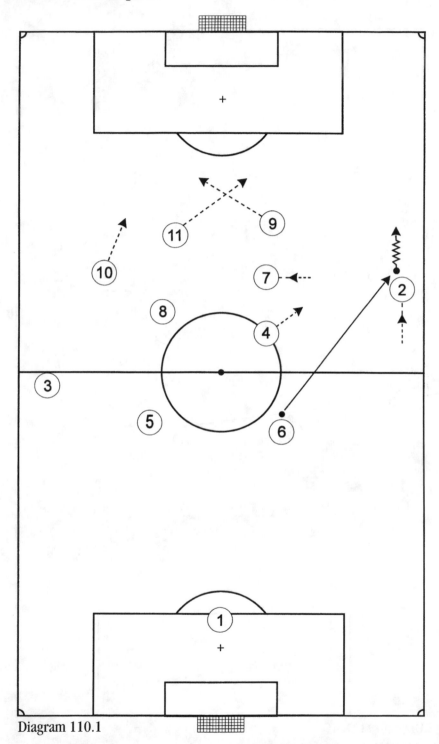

Diagram 110.1

**Scheme 7 first part**

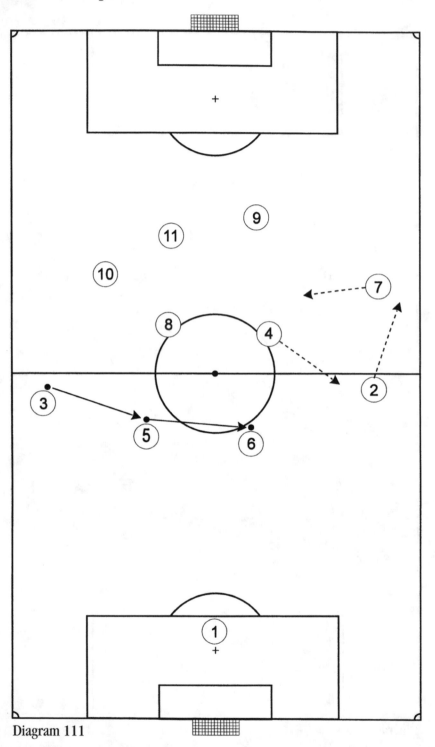

Diagram 111

Scheme 7 second part

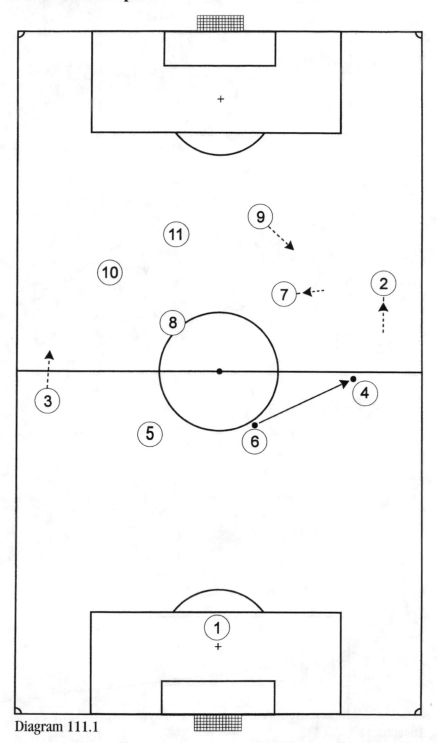

Diagram 111.1

## Scheme 8 first part

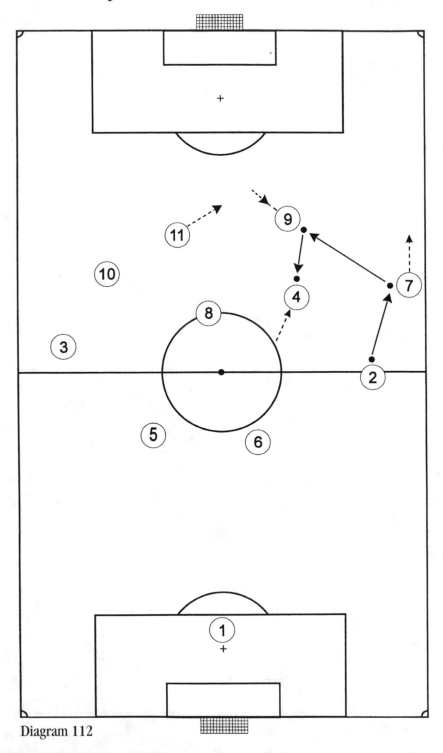

Diagram 112

# Scheme 8 second part

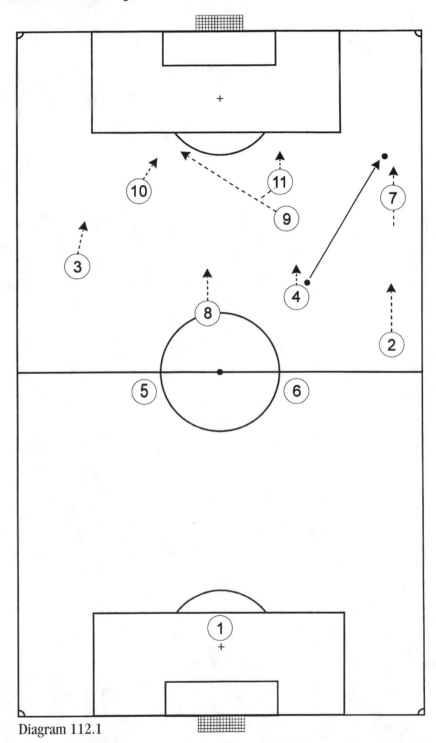

Diagram 112.1

# Scheme 9 first part

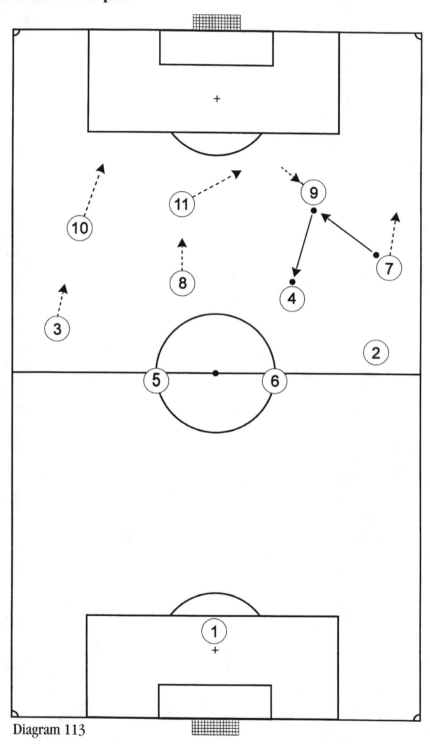

Diagram 113

# Scheme 9 second part

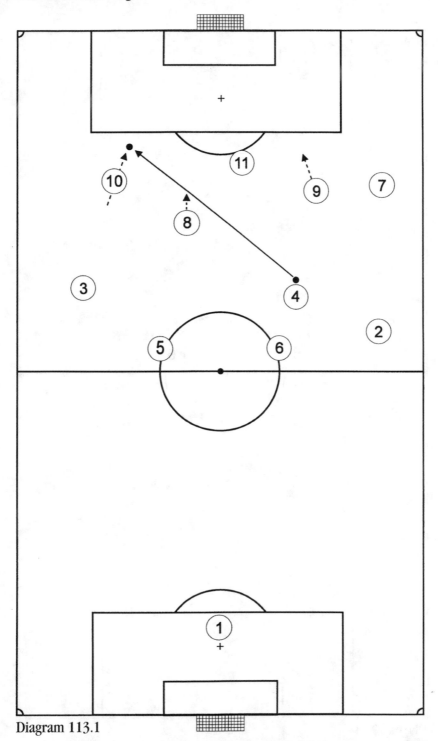

Diagram 113.1

## Scheme 10 first part

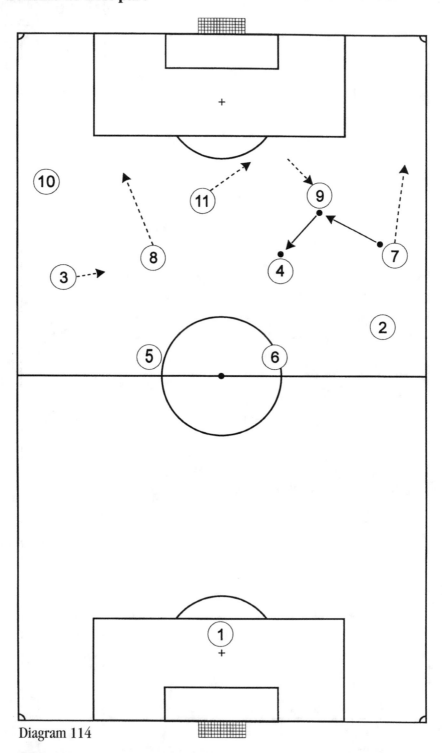

Diagram 114

# Scheme 10 second part

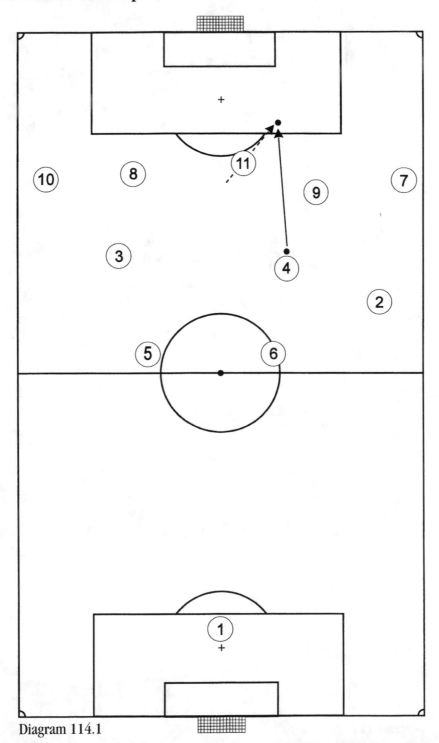

Diagram 114.1

# Scheme 11 first part

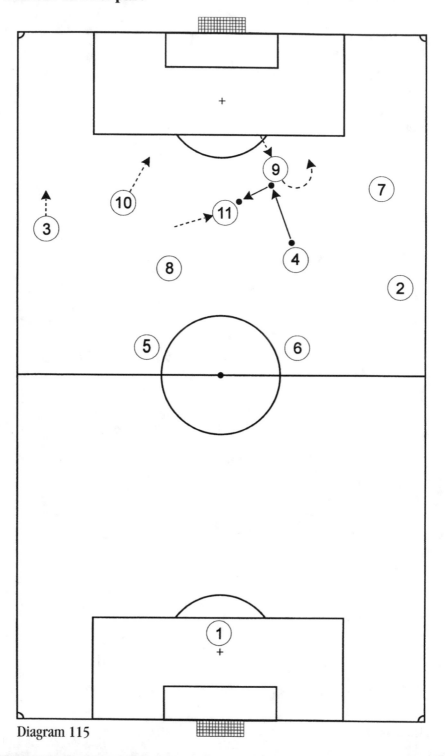

Diagram 115

Scheme 11 second part

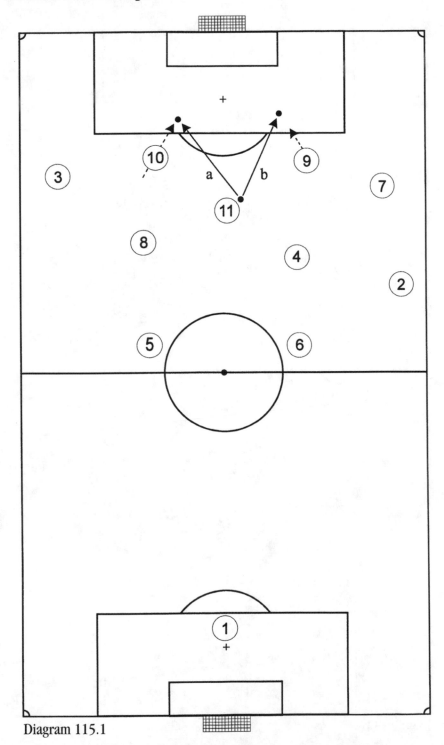

Diagram 115.1

# Scheme 12 first part

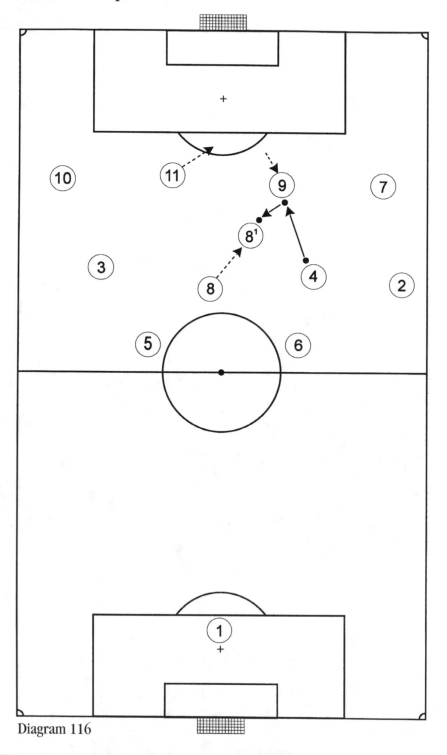

Diagram 116

# Scheme 12 second part

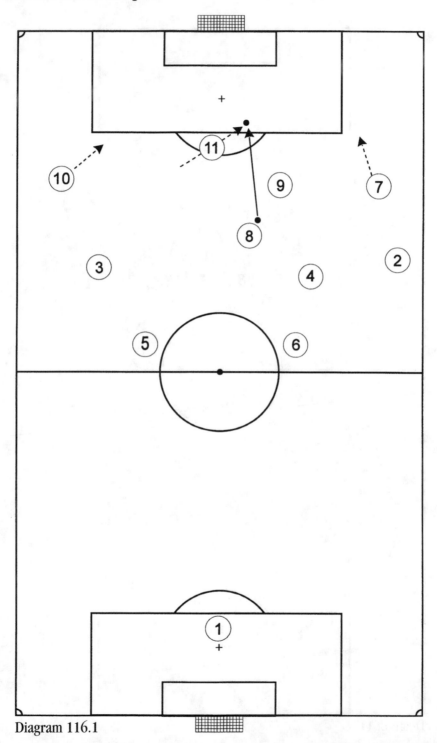

Diagram 116.1

**Scheme 13 first part**

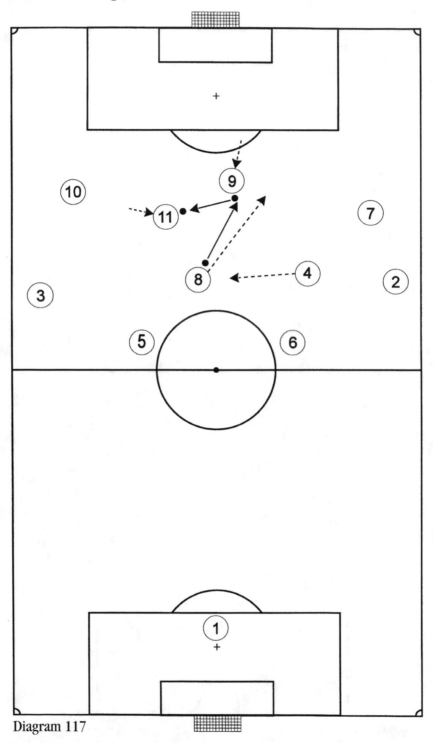

Diagram 117

## Scheme 13 second part

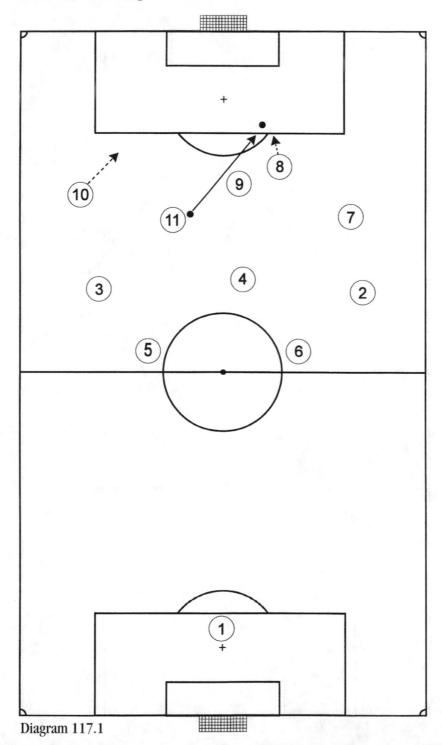

Diagram 117.1

# Scheme 14 first part

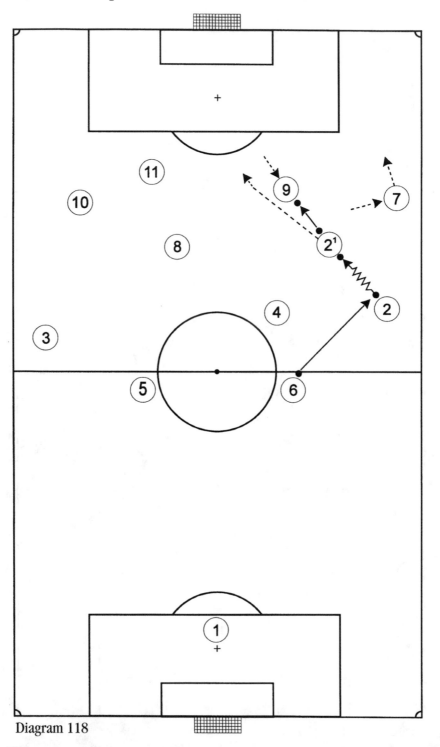

Diagram 118

## Scheme 14 second part

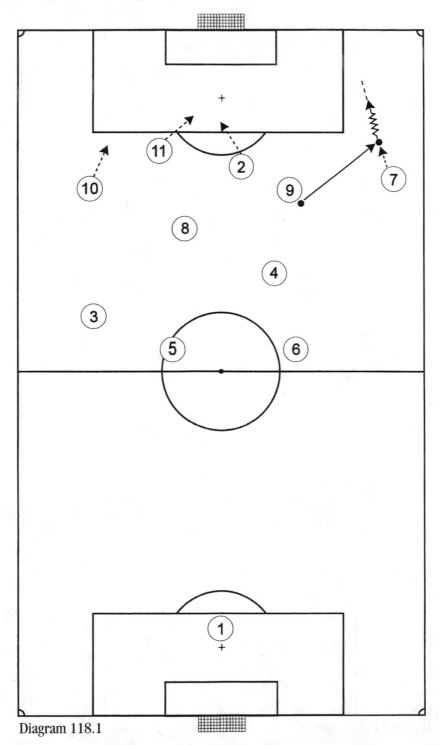

Diagram 118.1

**Scheme 15 first part**

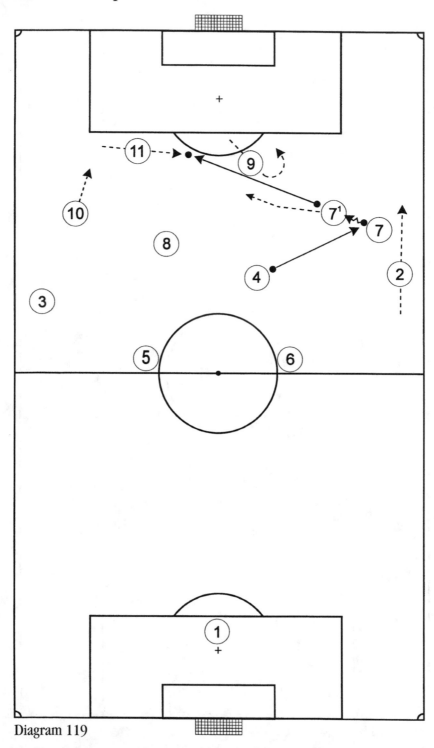

Diagram 119

**Scheme 15 second part**

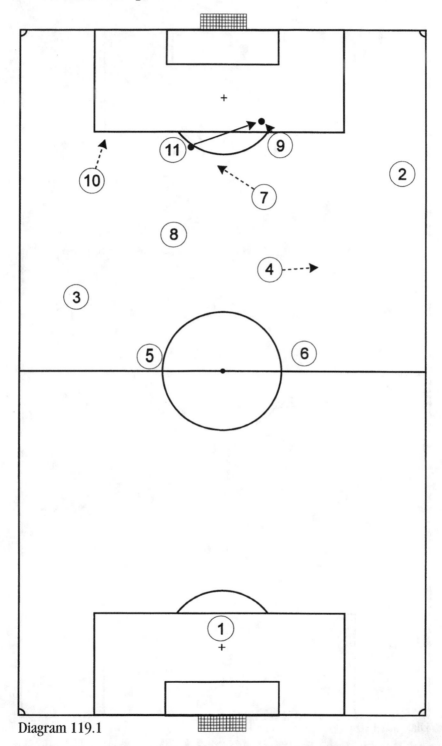

Diagram 119.1

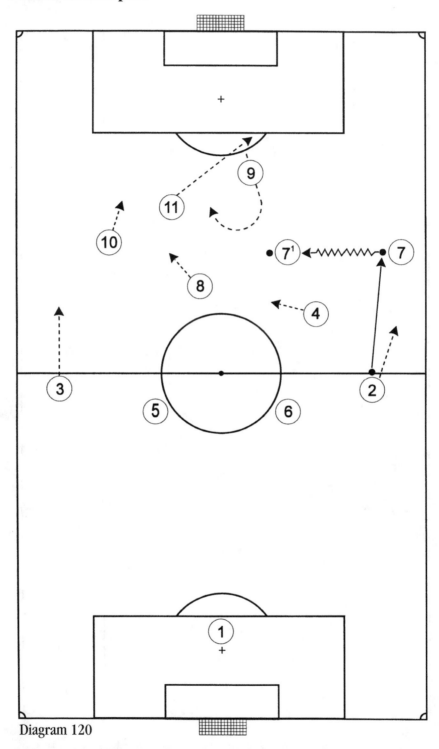

## Scheme 16 first part

Diagram 120

## Scheme 16 second part

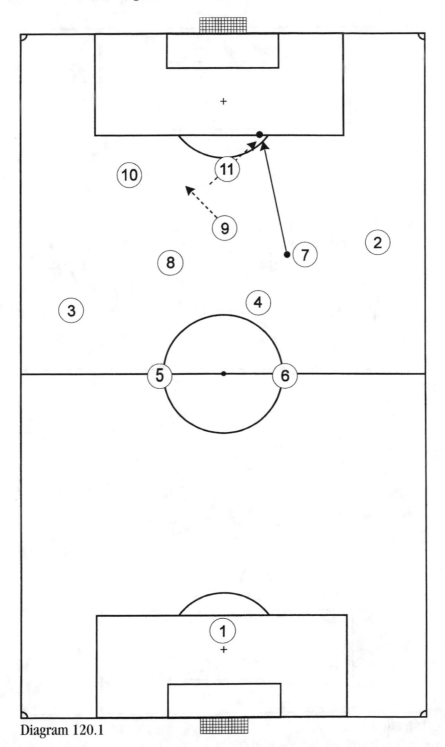

Diagram 120.1

# Scheme 17 first part

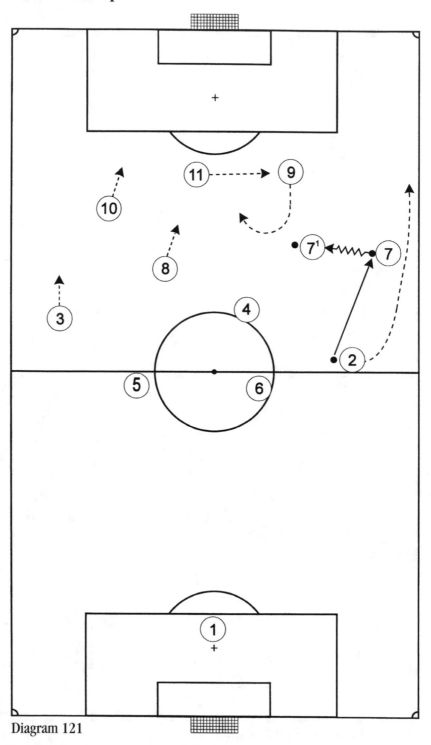

Diagram 121

# Scheme 17 second part

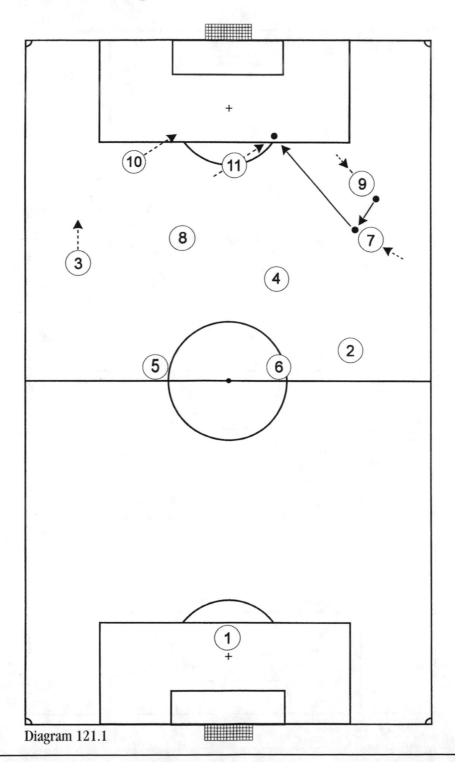

Diagram 121.1

# Scheme 18 first part

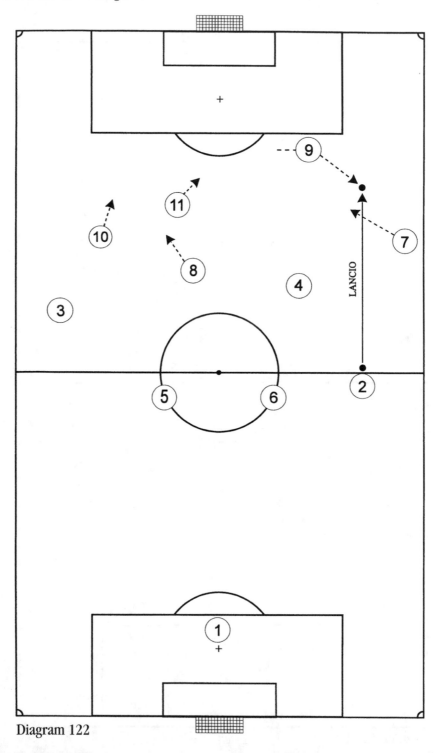

Diagram 122

## Scheme 18 second part

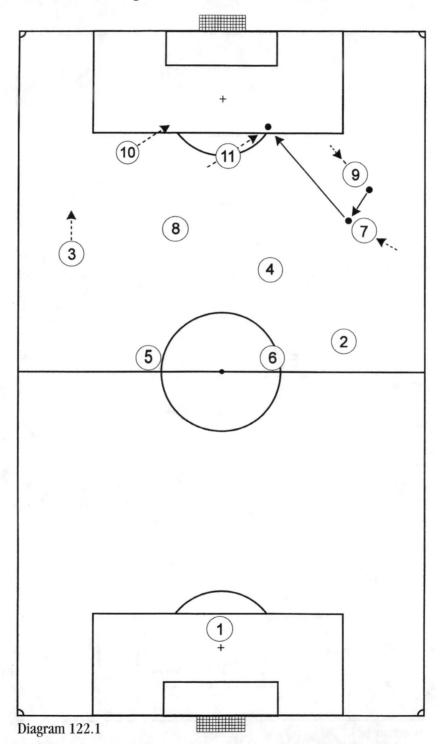

Diagram 122.1

# Scheme 19 first part

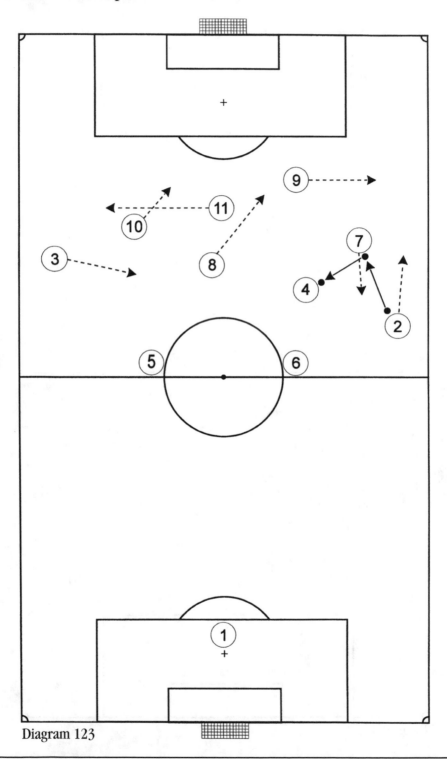

Diagram 123

# Scheme 19 second part

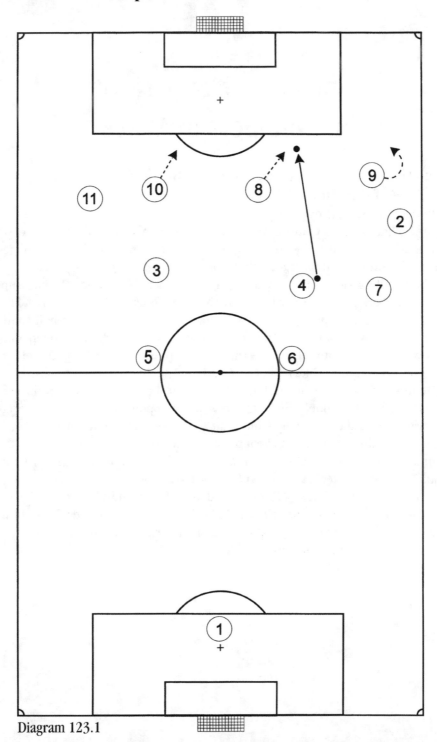

Diagram 123.1

# 10

# Situations of Superiority
# in Numbers in Attack

**Simulation of a Counterattack (3 v 2), with the Ball Intercepted in the Side Zone of the Midfield**

In diagram 124 the opposing team is attacking.

In this particular situation, that is with the team extended too far forward, while the ball is on its way from "B" to "C" our player number 7 manages to intercept it, throwing himself quickly towards the opposing penalty area.

The resulting situation (shown in diagram 124.1) is 3 versus 2, with superiority in numbers of the forwards with respect to the backs (numbers 7-9-11 versus "C" and "D"). In this situation, "C" attacks the player with the ball (number 7) trying to delay the attack, while "D" follows number 9 who runs deep, cutting ahead of the player with the ball. Number 11 is free from marking, therefore (as we can see in diagram 124.2) number 7 will choose the right time to pass him the ball, enabling him to run with it towards the opposing goal undisturbed. Generally, number 7 should make the pass when opponent "C", after playing for time, tries to take the ball away from him. At the very moment when "C" attacks number 7, number 11 should make a burst to receive the ball deep.

*In diagrams 124.1 and 124.2 we have not shown the other players because we have supposed that they were too late for the action.*

In diagram 124.1 back "D" has decided to follow number 9, but he could have also chosen to mark number 11. If he had done so, number 7 would have passed the ball to number 9 in depth, choosing the right time for the execution of the pass not to send his teammate off-side.

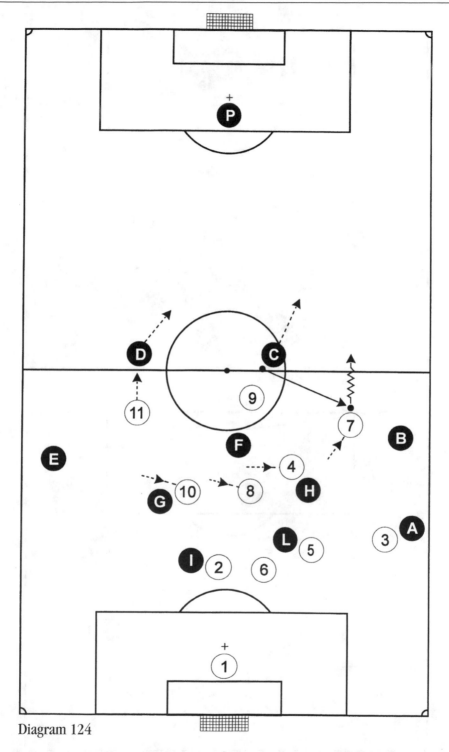

Diagram 124

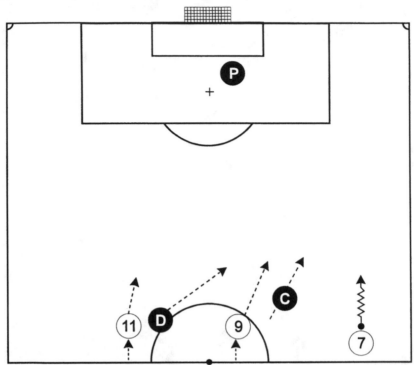

Diagram 124.1

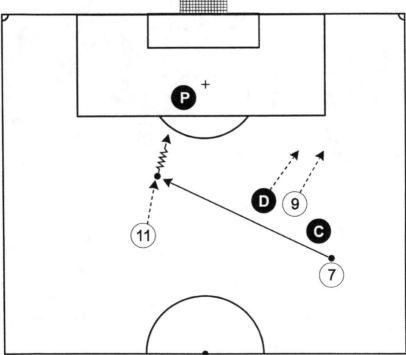

Diagram 124.2

## Simulation of a Counterattack (3 vs 2), with the Ball Intercepted in the Defensive Third

In diagram 125 the opposing team is attacking.

In this particular situation, that is with the team extended too far forward, while the ball is on its way from "C" to "F" our player number 4 manages to intercept it, throwing himself quickly towards the opposing penalty area.

The resulting situation (shown in diagram 125.1) *is 3 versus 2, with superiority in numbers of the forwards with respect to the backs* (numbers 4-9-11 versus "C" and "B"). In this situation, "C" must attack, playing for time, the player with the ball (number 4), while "B" follows number 9 who avoids cutting in to keep his marking opponent from going towards the center. The more the forwards play in narrow spaces, the fewer are the advantages from their superiority in numbers (3 versus 2) as the backs, given the short distances to cover, can re-arrange themselves according to the new forward with the ball, therefore a movement to the center by number 9 would be inappropriate.

Number 11 is free from marking, therefore (as we can see in diagram 125.2) number 4 will choose the right time to pass him the ball in depth, enabling him to run with it towards the opposing goal undisturbed.

It should be noticed that as soon as number 4 has passed the ball to number 11, the former overlaps the latter; this movement could turn out to be fundamental in case opposing back "C" managed to stop number 11.

*In diagrams 125.1 and 125.2 we have not shown the other players because we have supposed that they were too late for the action.*

In diagram 125.1 back "B" has decided to follow number 9, but he too could have chosen to mark number 4. If he had done so, number 4, before being pressed by the two opponents (therefore while "B" was going towards him) should have passed the ball to number 9 in depth, choosing the right time for the execution of the pass not to send his teammate off-side.

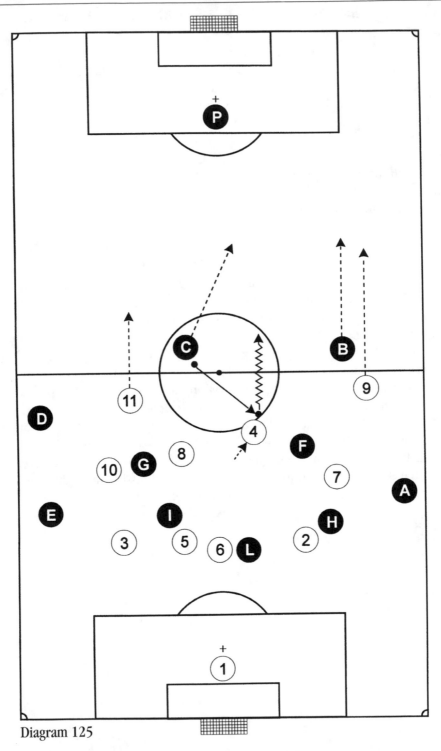

Diagram 125

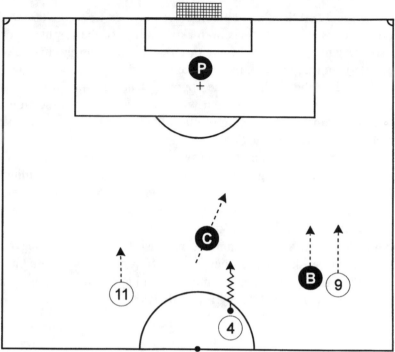

Diagram 125.1

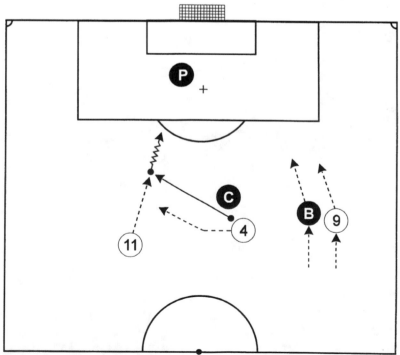

Diagram 125.2

## Conclusion

We have seen exercises and situations of play for training sessions during which little space is left to the decision-making ability of the single player.

In a soccer game, the times of shutting out, of marking gradually, of marking, of double-teaming, of marking in advance, of the application of the off-side trap, etc., depend on the choices of the opposing team; so the different exercises and situations which we have seen and which represent a cross-section of what can happen in a game are not enough to turn the "zone player" to the best decision to make in a particular situation.

In the zone play "situational training" is very important, it is also called "training through simplified games." Through such a system of training, reproducing the different situations which may occur in a game, inventiveness and responsibility are stimulated, along with a greater team spirit among the players; perceiving, analyzing, decision-making and executing abilities are also developed. Thanks to such situational games it is possible to produce a clever player, able to use the correct skills and tactics in the different situations of a game.

We should also not forget socio-emotional and aggression factors among the players which can be assessed through specific tests.

# BIBLIOGRAPHY

SIMONE MAZZALI        La zona nel calcio: Tecnica Tattica e Ruolo
                      Creativo
                      SOCIETA STAMPA SPORTIVA ROMA

HORST WEIN            Imparare il calcio
                      EDIZIONI MEDITERRANEE

SdS CONI              JANUSA EDITRICE S.r.l.


Il Nuovo Calcio       EDITORIALE SPORT ITALIA


Il Notiziario del Settore Tecnico F.I.G.C.

# More great soccer books
## *from REEDSWAIN*

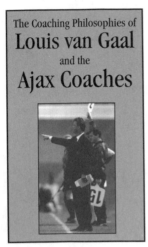

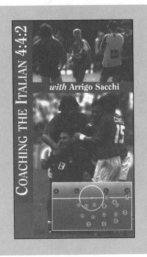